Questions and Answers On Family Law -- II (Muslim Law and other Personal Laws)

Questions and Answers

On

Family Law - II

(Muslim and other Personal Laws)

(Alongwith MCQs)

AND

Solved Practical Questions Part - C

BY

PROF. DR. REGA SURYA RAO,

(B.Com., M.L., Ph.D.)

ASSISTED BY

Mrs. Rega (Balivada) T. Gowri, B.Com., B.L.

ADVOCATE

LexWorth®

LexWorth®

This book is a publication of
Gogia Law Publication
Opposite High Court of Telangana,
Hyderabad 500 002.
Phones : (040) 24560631, 24525689
Email : lexworth@outlook.in

1ST Edition 2020

2ND Edition 2022

Reprint 2023

3RD Edition 2026

Typeset by : Khader Ahmed Khan

Printed by : Gogia Law Publications

DEDICATED TO
MY BELOVED WIFE

Late Mrs. Balivada (Rega)
Thirumala Gowri

B.Com., LL.B, Advocate

Who had been my great source of help and strength throughout my Academic Works

PREFACE

The subject, "Family Law in India" deals with the personal laws of different communities namely, Hindus, Mohammedans, Christians and other communities/religions. It is divided into two parts and prescribed for the study of LL.B. Three years and Five years Integrated course in two papers entitled "Family Law-I and Family Law-II. Some universities prescribed in the syllabus of Family Law-I, various concepts of Hindus *viz.* Marriage, Divorce, Adoption, Maintenance, Minority, Guardianship, Intestate and testamentary succession i.e. Family Law-I as Hindu Law and the said concepts in respect of Mohammedans in Family Law-II i.e. Muslim Law in India. However, some [illegible] prescribed the concepts of Marriage, Divorce, [illegible] Maintenance, Minority, Guardianship in respect of Hindus and Mohammedans in Family Law-I, while [illegible] of Intestate and Testamentary Succession [illegible] both Hindus and Mohammedan and other [illegible] the Special Marriage Act, 1954 the Indian [illegible] etc. are prescribed for study under Family Law-II.

This book titled "Family Law - II" (Muslim Law and other Personal Laws) covers all aspects of the Mohammedans namely Marriage, Divorce, Adoption, Maintenance, Minority, Guardianship, the laws of intestate succession and Testamentary succession, law of Wills, the Special Marriage Act, 1954 and the Indian Divorce Act, 1869.

I have dealt with the subject in as simple and lucid a way as possible in answering the best selected questions, keeping in mind, the requirement of students taking LL.B. Three years and Five years examinations.

PREFACE

The subject, "Family Law in India" deals with the personal laws of different communities namely, Hindus, Mohammedans, Christians and other communities/religions. It is divided into two parts and prescribed for the study of LL.B. Three years and Five years Integrated course in two papers entitled "Family Law-I and Family Law-II. Some universities prescribed in the syllabus of Family Law-I, various concepts of Hindus *viz.* Marriage, Divordce, Adoption, Maintenance, Minority, Guardianship, Intestate and testamentary succession *i.e.* Family Law-I as Hindu Law and the said concepts in respect of Mohemmedans in Family Law-II *i.e.* Muslim Law in India. However, some universities prescribed the concepts of Marriage, Divorce Adoption, Maintenance, Minority Guardianship in respect of the both Hindus and Mohammedans in Family Law-I, while the laws of Intestate and Testamentary Succession in respect of the both Hindus and Mohammedan and other legislations namely, the Special Marriage Act, 1954 the Indian Divorce Act, 1869 *etc.,* are prescribed for study under Family Law-II.

This book titled "Family Law - II" (Muslim Law and other Personal Laws) covers all aspects of the Mohammedans namely, Marriage, Divorce, Adoption, Maintenance, minority, Guardianship, the laws of satistate (Inheritence) and Teshamentary Succession (Law of Wills) the Special Marriage Act, 1954 and the Indian Divorce Act, 1869.

I have dealt with the subject in as simple and lucid a way as possible in answering the best selected questions keeping in mind, the requirement of students taking LL.B (Three years and Five years) examinations. An attempt is made in this work to enlighten the students to answer effectively and elaborately. I welcome suggestions and advice from legal scholars and students for improvement of this book.

With the great strength of encouragement and inspiration of my well wishers, I started writing law books in 1989, when I was a lecturer in law, Sir C.R.R Law College, Eluru, Andhra Pradesh, India. I published on my own two maiden ventures, Elements of Law of Torts and Outlines of Indian Legal and Constitutional History and study material (Notes) on 24 Law subjects, which received overwhelming response and drew the attention of the leading publishers in India viz., Asia Law House, Gogia Law Agency, Hyderabad and Andhra Law House, Vishakhapatnam. So far, more than 30 titles have been published. Most of them have been revised and more than 15 titles have been translated into Hindi.

I wish to express my profound gratitude to my eldest brother, Prof. Rega Jaganmohan Rao, Retd. Principal, University College of Law, Andhra University, Late Shri S. Prasada Rao, Retd. Joint Commissioner of Labour, A.P. Shri V. Bangar Raju, Retd. Chief Manager, Hindustan Shipyard Limited, Visakhapatnam, Late Dr. P. Koteswar Rao, Retd. Prof. of Law, S.V. University, Tirupati, Late. Dr. K. Vishnu Murty, Retd. Prof. of Law, K.U., Warangal (A.P.) Dr. N.S. Jagannadha Rao, LL.M., Ph.D., D. Lit. (Law), Retd. Prof. of Law, Berhampur University (Orissa), my research guide and the first recipient of D.Lit. in Law in the States of Orissa, Andhra Pradesh and some other States, my research guide Late Prof. B.S. Murty, Retd. Prof. of Human Resource Management, A.U., Late Shri

K. Jawaharlal, Member, Governing Body, Sir C.R.R. Institutions, Eluru, (A.P.), Smt. Vijayamala Raja Bhonsale, (Advocate, High Court of Mumbai), Adv. Shri Rameshchandra S. Bhonsale, Ex-Chairman, Phaltan Urban Co-op. Bank Ltd.), Shri Ranjit Singh R. Bhonsale, (Advocate, High Court of Mumbai), Chairperson, Secretary and Treasurer respectively of the Priyadarshini Dyan Probhodhini Sanstha's Law College, who are collectively and independently instrumental for what I am now.

I owe duty to thank my wife Late Mrs. Balivada T. Gowri, Advocate and my sons Srinivas Uday Kiran, B. Tech. (CSE), Srinivas Arun Kiran, III, Be. Tech. (Chem.), Software Engineers, but for whose encouragement and cooperation, I could not have been in a position to bring out the number of academic ventures on Law. I acknowledge my heartfelt thanks to Shri. Bharat Bhushan Gogia, Nirmit Gogia and Saksham Gogia of Gogia Law Agency for their encouragement and co-operation in getting this work published.

"Above all it must be hidden truth that the love, affection, blessings and benedictions of my beloved parents late Shri Rega Appa Rao and Smt. Kantha Ratnam, the sole reason for my gradual academic elevation".

--Prof. Dr. Rega Surya Rao

BLANK

QUESTIONS AND ANSWERS ON FAMILY LAW -- II

(MUSLIM AND OTHER PERSONAL LAWS)

CONTENTS

Unit -- I

Origin And Development Of Muslim Law

Question No. **Page No.**

UNIT -- II
DIVORCE

UNIT -- III

PATERNITY, GIFT AND WILL

UNIT -- IV

WAQF

UNIT -- V

INHERITANCE AND SUCCESSION

UNIT -- VI

OTHER PERSONAL LAWS

QUESTIONS AND ANSWERS ON FAMILY LAW -- II (MUSLIM LAW AND OTHER PERSONAL LAWS)

UNIT -- I

ORIGIN AND DEVELOPMENT OF MUSLIM LAW

Question No. 1

Write about the Concept and Background of Muslim Law ?

Answer :

There are mainly two different conception of Law, one of divine origin as in the case of Hindu Law, Muslim Law, etc. and another man-made. Muslim Law is founded upon revelation and is blended with religion.

There is in Islam a "Doctrine of Certitude" in the matter of good and evil. Human beings due to their weakness cannot understand what is good and evil, unless in the matter they are guided by the inspired prophet. What is morally beautiful, that must be done and what is morally ugly must not be done. That is Law of Shariat and nothing else can be law. This is the view of Muslim Jurists. In the words of Abdul

Rahim, Law is that which is established by a communication from God with reference to men's acts expressive either of demand or indifference on his part or being merely declaratory.

SHARIAT is law in the wider sense. It means the totality of God's commandment. Each one of such commandments is called HUKUM. It is a doctrine of duties. Legal considerations and individual rights have secondary place in it. SHARIAT says that religious injunctions are of five kinds. Those strictly enjoined are 'FARZ' and those strictly forbidden are 'HARAM'.

Law proper, in ISLAM, is FIQH (Jurisprudence) and it differs from 'Shariat. FIQH Literally sense intelligence and covers the whole science of jurisprudence. It implies the independent exercise of intelligence as regards points of law in the absence of their solution by the QURAN or 'HADIS. FIQH has been defined by the Muslim Jurists as 'the knowledge of one's right and obligation derived from Quran or Hadis or deduced therefrom or about which the learned have agreed.

Islamic conception of Law, Shariat and Fiqh, is connected with religion. Thus, the postulates of Muslim Jurisprudence are as follows :

(a) The first postulate is faith (Iman) in God and acknowledgement of His authority over our actions.

(b) The second is the belief in the prophethood of Mohammed.

God alone is the legislator in Islam and Quran in the Holy Law book. The authority to make laws primarily belongs to God and He alone has Supreme legislative power in the Islamic system.

The importance of the study of Muslim Law can be estimated from the fact that it is applicable to 425 million Muslims in 20 countries of Asia, Africa and Europe including more than 110 million Muslims in India and Pakistan. In other words, one-sixth of the total world population is following Islam. And if there is anything which is characteristic of and fundamental to that religion, it is the Sharia or the Muslim Law.

Question No. 2

Explain the various sources of Muslim Law and indicate their Relative Authority ?

Answer :

The following are the main and ancient sources of Muslim Law :

Sources of Muslim Law can be classified into two; i.e., sharia sources and Extraneous sources.

A. Sharia Sources

The following classifications of Sharia sources :

(1) The Quran

(2) Sunnah/Hadith (Tradition)

(3) IJMA (Consensus of opinion)

(4) QIYAS (Analogy)

(1) The Quran

According to Islamic theology, the Holy Book *i.e.,* The Quran is the only revealed book of ALLAH. The Quran is the fundamental source of Muslim Law. It contains about 6,000 verses but not more than 200 verses deal with legal principles. Of these 200 verses, there are about 80 verses which deal with the Law of Personal status. Most of them concerned with Inheritance, Marriage, Guardianship, Divorce, Dower, Wills, Gifts and such like matters. The Koran is not and does not profess to be a Code of Law or even a Law Book and the Prophet Mohammed was not a lawgiver but yet they interpret it as a Code. It would be a mistake to overlook its influence in shaping the Islamic legal principles. The Quran exercised this influence in Four different ways :

(a) Sometimes when the Prophet of Islam was faced with legal problems, he used to seek Divine guidance, and the answers which he received through Divine revelations formed a definite legal element in the holy Koran.

(b) Secondly, the non-legal texts of holy Koran which deal with morality and conscience have an effect on the legal science of Islam.

(c) It is stated in numerous texts of the Koran that the Law of God has also been revealed earlier. Therefore, it becomes probable that the early Muslims might have taken some help from other legal systems. For instance, Qiyas and logical deductions used by the Islamic lawyers have something common with the Jewish Legal system.

(d) The holy Quran gave the idea that law is the direct commandment of Allah. Since ALLAH is one, His law must be a single-whole, and in search for this single whole, the builders of the Islamic legal system have developed a very elaborate legal science.

(2) Sunnah/Hadith (Tradition)

The importance of Hadith or Sunnah as an important source of Muslim Law has been laid down in the holy Koran, emphasized by the Prophet recognized by his immediate successors and other companions and accepted by all important Muslim Jurists.

The successors of the Prophet followed the practice of the Prophet. If they did not know of any decision of the Prophet on a subject, they made enquiries from the companions about it and if any of them informed them of any Hadith on the subject, they decided the case accordingly. they, However, always tested the reliability of the Hadith *i.e.*, traditions. All the important orthodox Muslim jurist are unanimous in upholding the validity of Hadith or Sunnah as a source of Muslim Law.

However, Hadith (Sunnah) have been classified into the following three categories :

(a) Hadith Mutwatir (Continuous) : Those which have received universal acceptance and narrated by an indefinite number of men belonging to the categories of companions, successors and successors of successors.

(b) Hadith Mashhoor (Well-Known) : These were reported by a limited number of companions in the first instance and thereafter fulfilling the conditions of a continuous tradition.

(c) Hadith Ahad (Isolated) : These rest upon the testimony of one or more narrators, who are limited in number; not fulfilling the conditions of either of the above two classes.

(3) Ijma (Consensus Of Opinions)

The third source of Muslim Law is Ijma i.e., consensus of opinions. Ijma has been defined as the agreement of the Muslim juris consults in any particular age on a juridical rule. The authority of Ijma as a source of law is founded an Koranic and Sunnah texts.

Classification of Ijma

Ijma has been classified into three types : (a) Ijma of the companions of the Prophet;

(b) Ijma of the Jurists; and

(c) Ijma of the people.

While the first type is universally accepted and is incapable of being repealed, and the other two types are somewhat disputed.

The Shia school did not accept Ijma, on the other hand, Sunnis hold that since Koran enunciated only a few rules of law which after the death of the Prophet, who used to give guidance, are by no means sufficient to cover the numerous questions of day-to-day developments, Ijma becomes necessary in the circumstances.

Ijma may be constituted by decision expressed in words or by practice. Both are equally authoritative.

Requirements of Ijma : A few of the important requirements for the validity of Ijma. They are :

(a) It shall not come into conflict with Koran or Hadith.

(b) Once a question is determined by Ijma, it cannot be re-opened by individual jurists.

(c) One Ijma may be reversed by a subsequent Ijma; and

(d) When the jurists of an age have expressed only two views on a particular question, a third view is inadmissible.

Ijma has made a worthy contribution to Islamic law in as much as it has made possible changes to suit the needs of changing times and usages, and in as much as it has been influenced by the opinions of jurists in all cases not provided for in the Koran or the traditions *i.e.;* Hadith or Sunnah.

(4) Qiyas (Analogy) : Qiyas *i.e.*; Analogy is the last source of Muslim Law. It is a process of deduction by which the law of a text is applied to cases which though not covered by the language are governed by the reason of the text. Hanifi law defines it as; "an extension of law from the original text to which the process is applied to a particular case by means of a common Illat or effective cause, which cannot be ascertained merely by interpretation of the language of the text".

All the four schools of the Muslim Law accept the authority of Qiyas as a source of law but the Shias do not recognise it.

(B) Extraneous sources : Those sources which have not been mentioned by the classical jurists but which have an impact in the evolution of Muslim Law, are termed as "Extraneous sources. These sources are the direct legislation by the state, custom and usages and legal fiction.

(1) Legal Fiction : In Islamic Law there are some instances of legal fiction. The inhabitants of Bukhava had been accustomed to long term leases of land. But as the Hanafi school did not approve long lease contracts for orchards, recourse was made to a legal fiction where by the orchards was sold and the vendor retained. The right to redeem it. This form of sale was obviously a legal fiction to the circumvent the prohibition of long lease contracts. Mahamassini gives many other such examples and shows that legal fiction can also be a source of Law, and this source is approved by Hanafis and some Shafies only, while Makili, Hanbalis and a majority of shafies do not approve of it.

(2) Legislation : The history of the Islamic states shows that the Caliphs and the Sultans enacted Laws either directly or indirectly whenever public interest called for such action. The legality of such legislation is totally based on Quran and Hadith *i.e.* tradition.

(3) Customs : Before the advent of Islam in Arabia, customs were the basis of the entire social life, religion, morality, trade and commerce, and no codified law existed. But there were customs of marriage, dower, inheritance, gifts, wills, etc. All such pre-Islamic and ancient customs which were beneficial for the community got recognition in religion after the advent of Islam. Koran is the fundamental source of Muslim Law. but at the time the custom can also be not neglected. As a result, the customs are accepted as supplementary to the sacred law. In India, the courts clearly recognized the customs.

Question No. 3

Discuss the various schools of Muslim Law ?

Answer :

The major sources of Muslim law include the Quran, Sunna, Hadis, Ijma as well as Qiya. Qiya refers to interpretations of Muslim jurists on matters that neither the Quran nor Sunna explains.

Since it was inevitable for jurists to interpret all sources differently, conflicting interpretations often emerged. Consequently, these differences of opinions led to the creation of various schools of law.

Sunnis and Shias are the two main sects of Islam and both of these sects have their own schools. Although there are differences of opinions amongst these schools, the Muslim world considers all of them to be correct. Thus, no school has more prominence over another.

(a) Sunni Schools (Sects)

Following are the main schools of Sunni sects :

(1) The Hanafi school (701 A.D. to 705 A.D.)

(2) The Maliki school (718 A.D. to 795 A.D.)

(3) The Shafei school (768 A.D. to 827 A.D.)

(4) The Hanbali school (802 A.D.)

(1) The Hanafi School : This is the most important of the Four Schools of the Sunnis. Its founder was the Great Imam Abu Hanifa. The main features of this school are :

(a) Less reliance on Hadith or sunnah (traditions)

(b) Greater reliance on Qiyas i.e; reasoning and analogy.

(c) A less scope of Ijma (Consensus of openions)

(d) The Doctrine of Jurestic Equity (Istehsan) was also introduced.

The primary authorities of this school were Abu Hanifi Abu Yusuf and Imam Mohammed (Last two authorities were most famus disciples of Abu Hanifa.

This school is followed in Egypt, Turkey, Lebenon, Syria, Afghanistan, India, Pakistan, China, etc. Its adherents constitute more than one-third of the Muslims of the world.

(2) The Maliki School : This school was founded by Imam Malik. The main distinctions of this school are as follows :

(a) This school gave more stress on sunnah *i.e;* tradition, and if there was a conflict between the tradition, the Ijma was resorted.

(b) The analogical deductions (Qiyas) were also not ruled out.

(c) The power of the head of the family over his wife's property or over children.

This school is still predominant in Moracco, Algeria, Tunisia, Kuwait, Behrain, Sudan, etc.

(3) The Shafei School : The founder of this school was Imam Shafei. This school was a compromise between the Hanafi and Maliki schools. The Imam Shafei was the first to compile the sources of Muslim Law. This school founded the Doctrine of Qiyas which might be based on Koran, Hadith (Sunna) or Ijma. The reliance on Sunna (Traditions) was given by this school more than Abu Hanifa but less than Imam Malik. This school is followed in many parts of Egypt, Syria, Lebnon, Iraq, Pakistan, India, Indo-China, Java, Iran (Sunni inhabitants) and Yemen). It is predominant in Jordan and Palistine.

(4) The Hanbali School : The founder of the fourth Sunni School is Imam hanbal. He is more strict follower of the Sunnah (traditions) than others and restricted Qiyas and Ijma within narrow limits. The foundation of this school rests on Five main sources :

(a) Quran

(b) The Sunnah (Tradition)

(c) The Ijma of the companions of the prophet

(d) Zaif and Mursal traditions *i.e.,* traditions having a weak chain of transmission

(e) Qiyas, whenever it was necessary.

This school, today, is the official school of the Kingdom of Saudi Arabia, and has followers in the Arabian Peninsula, Palestine, Syria, Iraq and other countries.

(B) Shia Schools (Sects) : Following are the main sub-schools.

(1) Athna Asharia school

(2) Ismailiya school

(3) Zaidya school

(1) Athna Asharia School : This is the largest sub-school of the Shia School. There were twelve Imams that is why they were called Twelvers. This school was sub-divided into 'Akbari' and 'Usuli' school. The Akabari school was rigid traditionalists while the Usuli school believed in the free scope of human reasons in the interpretation of Koran, the genuiness of traditions by their confirmity of Koranic spirit.

The AthnaAsharia school prevails in Lebanon, Iran Iraq, Pakistan and India also.

(2) Ismailya school : The followers of Ismail are called Ismailyas. They believe that there were only seven Imams not twelve Imams and Ismail was the seventh Imam. They believe that from Ismail descended a series of concealed Imams. The Ismailyas are found in Central Asia, Syria, India and Pakistan.

(3) Zaidiyah School : The Shias became divided into sub-sections on the question of succession after the fourth imam, A1:Zain-ul-Abidin. One of his sons, Zayd was accepted as imam by a certain group who were called the 'Zaidis'. The recognise the principle of election as the basis of succession.

The Zaidis are found in Pakistan and India : Other schools

Besides the schools under Shia and Sunni sects, there are some other schools which are also present which are:

Ibadi School : Ibadi is a school which belongs neither to the Shia nor Sunni sect and this school claim that its history traces back to the times of 4th Khaleefa Ali. The Ibadi school gives more preference to the Quran and they do not give the Sunna much importance. This school has its followers in Oman. One of the most important points about this school is that besides the Quran, it has provided principal consideration to Ijtihad (personal reasoning) which has been partially accepted by the Sunnis and has been completely rejected by the Shias.

Ahmadiya School : The followers of Ahmadiya school claim to be Muslims but they do not follow Prophet Muhammed. This school has a recent origin and they are followers of one Ahmed who was alive in the 19th century.

This school is said to have a British-Indian origin and Mirza Ghulam Khadiani is the founder of this school, who served the British Government. Even though this school claims to be a follower of Islam, none of the Muslim Government has accepted them as Muslims because they believe this school's faith is completely against the faith of Muslims.

The Khadiyan village which is situated in Punjab in India is said to be the birthplace of Ahmed and thus it is their holy place and the followers are also known as Kadhiyani. There is no authoritative book of this school and because its origin is also recent, it has no recognition by the other authoritative books of Islam.

There are many differences between the Ahmadiya School and Muslims therefore, they are not regarded as part of Islam. The major points of difference between them are as follows:

1. The Muslims believe that Prophet Mohammad was the Messenger of God on Earth and he was the last Prophet who had spoken with God. Thus, his teachings are an important part of the lives of Muslims but the Ahmadiyas believe that God still communicates with his holy servants even after Prophet Mohammad.

2. The Ahmadiyans claim that the list of Prophets before Mohammad includes Buddha, Krishna, Zoroaster and Ramchandra and they claim it is according to the Quran but the non-Ahmadiyans do not accept such claims and refuse to acknowledge them as Prophets.

3. Unlike the Muslims, the Ahmadiyans do not accept the claim of the Sultan of Turkey as the Caliphate and they claim that every Muslim person should remain loyal to the Government of their country.

4. While Muslims believe that Mahdi will have a holy war or Jihad and Islam will be spread by the sword, the Ahmadiyas believe that it will be spread by arguments and heavenly signs and not through violence.

Question No. 4

State the difference between Sunni and Shia Schools?

Answer :

Sunni and Shia Muslims share the most fundamental Islamic beliefs and articles of faith and are the two main sub-groups in Islam. Difference between Sunni and Shia has originated from political and spiritual grounds. The other differences are on the basis of religious practices and rituals people follow. Sunni is an Arabic word which means the one who follows the traditions or Sunah of the Prophet whereas Shia word is derived from Shiayat e Ali that means friends of Ali.

Sunni (Hanafi) Law	Shia Law
1. Imamat	
The Sunnis regard the successor of the Prophet as the *Khalifa* or Caliph, who is 'a temporal ruler' rather than a religious chief. The Prophet is an ordinary mortal elevated to the high office on account of his qualifica-	The Shias regard the Imam as the final interpreter of the law on earth. He is a descendant of the Prophet, Ali and is the leader by Divine Right.

Sunni (Hanafi) Law	Shia Law
tion. In religious matters he has simply to follow the path of *Shariat*.	
2. Marriage	
(i) A temporary marriage i.e., *muta* which is a marriage for a limited period containing stipulations as to dower and period of time is not lawful amongst the Sunnis	*Muta* marriages are lawful among the Shias
(ii) Amongst the Sunnis there is a long list of other guardians for the purpose of marriage besides the father and grandfather who can act as *wali-ul-nikah,* they being father, father's father how high soever, brother other paternal relations, mother, maternal uncle, etc.	Under Shia law only the father and grandfather can act as legal guardians *i.e., wali-ul-nikah* for purpose of marriage, others being regarded as Fazuli or unauthorized persons. Marriages contracted by such unauthorized person are naturally without any legal efect, unless ratified by party concerned on attaining puberty

Sunni (Hanafi) Law	Shia Law
(iii) Sunni (Hanafi) law prescribes the presence of two male witnesses at the time of marriage	Shia law does not prescribed the the presence of two male witnesses at the time of marriage
(iv) Two witnesses are not necessary at the time of dissolutionof marriage among Sunnis	Presence of two witnesses is essential at the time of dissolution of marriage among Shias
(v) The Sunni law recognizes the doctrine of valid retirement *i.e.,* the presumption of the consummation of marriage if the husband and wife retire into the nuptial chamber and there is no impediment to sexual intercourse	The Shia law does not recognize the doctrine of valid retirement so as to amount to consummation of marriage
(vi) Marriage can be cancelled on the ground of inequality between the two parties amongst sunnis	Marriage cannot be cancelled on the ground of inequality between the two parties

Sunni (Hanafi) Law	Shia Law
(vii) The Sunnis hold two years as the period of gestation	The Shias hold ten months as the longest period of gestation
(viii) Under the Sunni law a child born within two years of the termination of marriage is presumed to be legitimate	Under the Shia law, the child will be presumed legitimate only if born within ten months from the dissolution of marriage
(ix) Remarriages after the third triple repudiation are legalized amongst Sunnis	Remarriage after the third triple repudiation is never legalized amongst Shias
(x) Generally the Mahomedan law does not validate a marriage of man with his foster-sister as there is an absolute prohibition to marriage arising from fosterage, which is the relationship through nursing and suckling. But, the Sunni law excludes some foster relations from absolute prohibition	The Shia law does not recognized the exceptions permitted by the Sunnis regarding the marriage arising from fosterage

Sunni (Hanafi) Law	Shia Law
with whom a valid marriage may be contracted. They are sister's foster-mother, foster-sister's mother, foster-son's, sister, foster-child's grandmother, foster-child's aunt etc.	
(xi) Under Sunni (Hanafi) law, marriages are divided into valid, invalid and irregular marriages	Under Shia law, marriages, are either valid or void
3. Dower	
(i) The Sunni law recognizes ten dirhams as the minimum amount of dower	The Shia law does not fix any minimum limit of dower
(ii) There is no upper limit of dower in Sunni law	Shia law recognized 500 dirhams as the proper dower. Presumption or 500 dirhams as the maximum in case there is no stipulation
(iii) According to Sunni law, where there is no agree-	In Shia law, if there is no stipulation, at the time of

Sunni (Hanafi) Law	Shia Law
ment between parties, the rule is to regard part as prompt and part as deferred, the proportion of each being determined with due regard to custom, status of the parties and the amount of dower settled	marriage whether dower is to be prompt or deferred the whole of it is presumed as prompt
4. Divorce	
(i) Under Sunni law a talak may be oral or in writing.	Under Shia law a *talak* must be pronounced *orally* in Arabic language if there is ability to do so and in the presence and hearing of two reliable male Muslim witnesses. It cannot be effected in writing unless the husband is physically unable to pronounce it orally. Even an absent person cannot effect a talak in writing in Shia law.
(ii) Under Sunni law express words are necessary to	In Shia law talak pronounced in implied or ambiguous

	Sunni (Hanafi) Law	Shia Law
	convey the idea of divorce. If the words are ambiguous, then it will be necessary to prove that a talak was clearly intended.	terms will have no effect whether there was an intention to divorce or not. Divorce is not void if proved it was clearly intended
(iii)	If the words of divorce used by husband are express under Sunni law, the divorce is valid even if pronounced in jest, in a state of voluntary intaxication or under compulsion of threats of a serious nature.	Under Shia law, divorce under compulsion or threats or in intoxication in void.
(iv)	Under Sunni law no option can be reserved in a divorce and a divorce pronounced subject to an opinion will take effect immediately the option being regarded as void	Under the Shia law the talak itself in circumstances of option is void and produces no effect
(v)	The Sunni law recognized a *talak-ul-biddat* completely	Under Shia law the pronouncement of divorce must be strictly in accordance with

Sunni (Hanafi) Law	Shia Law
	the Sunna, and consequently a *talak-ul-biddat* which becomes effective as soon as it is pronounced is not valid
5. Maternity Maternity of the child, under Sunni law, is established in the woman who gave birth to the child whether by fornication (*Zina*) or by valid marriage	Under Shia law, a child born of fornication is deemed to have no mother at all and the maternity of a child born to a woman who was validly married before conception is established in the woman
6. Guardianship Under Sunni law, mother is entitled tot he custody of the boy upto seven years and a girl until she attains puberty	Under Shia law, the mother is entitled to the custody of boy to two years and a girl upto seven years
7. Maintenance (i) Under the Sunni law, it is obligatory to maintain father even if he is able to earn himself	Under the Shia law, it is not obligatory to maintain father if he is able to earn

	Sunni (Hanafi) Law	Shia Law
(ii)	Under the Sunni law, the liabiity of maintenance is shared equally by his children	Under the Shia law, in case thre are more persons than one who are liabel to maintain, the burden is shared according to the means and ability of each
8.	**Waqf**	
(i)	Under Sunni law a waqf inter vivos is completed by a mere declaration an endowment by the owner	Under the Shia law such a waqf is invalid unless accompanied by delivery of possession. Mere declaration of endowment is not enough.
(ii)	Under Sunni law, the settler may provide for his own maintenance and support duering his lifetime or for the payment of his debts out of the rents and profits of the property dedicated	Under the Shia law, a provision for the payment of personal debts of the waqf is not permissible and will make the wakf invalid
9.	**Wills**	
(i)	Under Sunni law, consent of the heirs is	Under Shia law, a person is an absolute owner of the one-

Sunni (Hanafi) Law	Shia Law
essential to validate a bequeth	third of his estate and can bequeth that one-third without the consent of the other heirs. If the legacy exceeds one-third, it is not valid even under the Shia law unless the other heirs consent thereto
(ii) Under Sunni law, the legacy lapses, in case of the legatee's death in the lfietime of the testator	Under Shia law, in case of the legatee's death in the lifetime of the testator, the legacy passes to his heirs unless is revoked by the testator
10. Gift	
Under the Sunni law, a gift of undivided share in teh property is invalid if it is incapable of partition	Under Shia law, a gift of undivided share inthe property is valid provided, it is capable of partition
11. Pre-emption	
Under the Sunni law, besides a co-sharer, a participation in the appendages or an owner	Shia law, recognizes the right of pre-emption only in case of co-sharers and that wo if the member does not exceed two

Sunni (Hanafi) Law	Shia Law
of the property inthe vicinity can also claim the right of pre-emption.	
12. Inheritance	
i) Under Sunni law there are three classes of heirs, namely (a) sharers; (b) residuaries and (c) distant kindred	Under Shia law, there are only two classes of heirs namely (i) sharers and (ii) residuaries
ii) The doctrine of primogeniture is not recognized	Under Shia law, according to the law of the primogeniture, the eldest son gets the deceased father's garment, the signet-ring, the sword and the Quran
iii) There is such distinction between real and personal property and the childless widow can inherit even the immovable property	A Shia childless widow is not permitted to take any share in her husband's immovable property

Sunni (Hanafi) Law	Shia Law
iv) Both husband and wife can take *by return*	Only the husband and not the wife is entitled *to return*
v) A man is excluded from inheritance when the murder was either intentional or unintentional	Under Shia law, a man is excluded from inheritance if he intentionally caused the murder of the person whom he is going to inherit.

Question No. 5

What do you understand about Shariat and Fiqh- Distinguish between them ?

Answer :

There are two different conceptions of law. One is that law is divine like Hindu and Muslim law, and the other is that law is man-made, such as all the modern legislation.

Shariat (the path to be followed) as a technical term; thus means "the canon law of Islam", embracing all human actions. It is more ethics than law. It is fundamentally a doctrine of duties, a Code of obligations. It gives more weight to a religious evaluation of all the affairs of life.

Fiqh literary means intelligence. It is the name given to the whole science of jurisprudence, because it implies the independent exercise of intelligence in deciding a point of law.

Muslim Jurists define Fiqh as, "the knowledge of one's right and obligation derived from the Quran or Hadith or deduced therefrom or about which the learned have agreed.

From the above definition it is clear that the science of Muslim law or Fiqh is based on Quran and Hadith (Sunnah) and Qiyas (Analogical deduction). The Ijma or consensus of opinion among the learned, is also a source of Fiqh.

Distinction between Shariat and Fiqh : Shariat is a wider circle, it embraces in its orbits all human actions, whether legal or otherwise, whereas Fiqh is the narrower circle, and deals with legal acts. Shariat owes its existence to the Koran and Hadith (sunnah), while Fiqh is mainly erected by human endeavour. In other words, the path of Shariat is laid down by God and His Prophet Mohammed. In the Fiqh, an action is either legal or illegal. In the Shariat there are various grades of approval or disapproval.

Question No. 6

Who is a Muslim ? What is the effect of conversion to Islam by a person on his rights of inheritance and his marital rights ?

Answer :

Any person who profess the Muslim religion, that is, acknowledges (1) that there is but one God, and (2) that Mohammed is his Prophet, is a Muslim. Such a person may be a Muslim by birth, or he may be a Muslim by conversion. It is not necessary that he should observe any particular rites or ceremonies or be an orthodox believer in that religion; no court can test or gauge the sincerity of religious belief. It is sufficient if he professes the Muslim religion in the sense that he accepts the unity of God and the prophetic character of Mohammed.

The view point of Law court in regard to a Muslim is as follows:

"Every person who believes in the unity of God and the mission of Mohammed as a Prophet is a Muslim to whatever sect he may belong".

The above said view point was given in the case of *Jiwan Khan vs. Habibi,* AIR 1933 Lah. 159 and it was also held that Shias are Muslims.

Effect of Conversion : (a) *On Inheritance :* Succession to the estate of convert to Islam is governed by Muslim Law.

According to Muslim law, a Hindu cannot succeed to the estate of Muslim. Therefore, if a Hindu, who has a Hindu wife and children, embraces Islam and marries a Muslim wife and has children by her, his property will pass on his death to his Muslim wife and children, and not to his Hindu wife or children.

(b) *On Marital Rights :* The conversion of his Hindu wife to Islam does not *ipso facto* dissolve her marriage with her husband. She cannot, therefore, during his life time enter into a valid contract of marriage with any other person. Thus, if she, after conversion to Islam, goes through a ceremony of marriage with a Muslim, she will be guilty of bigamy under Section 494 of the Indian Penal Code. (*Govt. of Bombay vs. Ganga,* (1880) 4 Bom. 330).

According to Muslim Law, a distinction is made between conversion to Islam of one of the spouses when such conversion takes place.

(i) in a country subject to Muslim Law, and

(ii) in a country where the law of Islam is not the law of the land.

In the first case, when one of the parties converts to Islam, she or he should offer to the other party to convert to Islam. If the other party refuses to do so, the marriage can be dissolved.

In the second case, the marriage is automatically dissolved after the lapse of the period of three months after the adoption of Islam by one of the spouses.

In India, the spouse who has embraced Islam cannot file a suit for divorce or for declaration that the marriage is dissolved against the spouse who refuses to embrace the Islam.

Under Section 4 of the Dissolution of Muslim Marriage Act, 1939, the apostacy of the Muslim wife does not automatically dissolve her marriage. This section provides that the renunciation of Islam by a Muslim Married woman or her conversion to a faith other than Islam shall not by itself operate to dissolve her marriage.

Provided that the provisions of this section shall not apply to a woman converted to Islam from some other faith who re-embraces her former faith.

Question No. 7

Explain the concept of Marriage in Muslim Law and state the essentials of Muslim marriage ?

Answer :

Under Muslim Law, marriage is a purely civil contract and not a sacrament. Justice Mahmood observed in the case of *Abdul Qadir vs. Salima,* (8 All. 149) that the "the marriage is a civil contract, upon the completion of which, by proposal and acceptance, all the rights and obligations, which it creates, arise immediately and simultaneously". It is thus an agreement between the parties the terms where of depend on the will of the consenting parties. Like other contracts, it is constituted by a proposal made by one or on behalf of one of the parties to the marriage, and an acceptance of the proposal by or on behalf of the other. Such contracts must be accompanied by dower, which is price paid to the wife for the connubial rights of the husband.

Definitions of valid marriage : The following definitions given by different scholars and jurists:

(1) Mullah : Marriage (Nikah) is defined to be a contract which has for its object the procreation and the legalizing of children.

(2) Hedaya : Marriage is a legal process by which the sexual intercourse and procreation and legitimation of children between man and woman is perfectly lawful and valid.

(3) Justice Mahmood : Marriage among muslims is not a sacrainent, but purely a civil contract.

(4) Abdur Rahim : The Muslim jurists regard the institution of marriage as partaking both of the nature of ibadat (devotional acts) and maamulat (Dealings among men).

(5) M.B.S. Jung : Marriage though essentially a contract is also a devotional act. Its objects are rights of enjoyment and procreation of children and regulation of social life in interest of society.

Classification of Marriages : Muslim marriage can be classified as follows :—

(1) Valid

(2) Void and

(3) Irregular or Invalid

(1) Valid Marriage : A valid marriage is one which conforms in all respects with the legal requirements and there should be no prohibition affecting the parties.

(2) Void Marriage : A marriage which has no legal results is termed as void. A marriage forbidden by the rules of blood relationship, affinity or fosterage is void. Similarly, a marriage with the wife of another or remarriage with a divorced wife without observing strict rules set for this occasion, is void.

(3) Irregular or Invalid : A marriage may be either lawful or unlawful. Unlawfulness may be either absolute or relative. If the unlawfulness is absolute, the marriage is void. If it is relative, it is an irregular marriage.

The following are irregular marriages :

(a) A marriage without witnesses.

(b) A marriage with a woman undergoing Iddat.

(c) A marriage prohibited by reason of difference of religion.

(d) A marriage with two sisters at the same time

(e) A marriage with a fifth wife.

Under shia law, all the above irregular marriages are treated as void, because shia law does not recognize the distinction between irregular and void marriages. A marriage is, according to that system either valid or void.

The issues of an irregular marriage are treated as legitimate and are entitled to inherit. But there are no rights of inherits between the husband and the wife. The wife is entitled to dower if the marriage is consummated, and has to observe Iddat for three courses (three Lunar months).

Essentials of valid marriage :

The following are the essentials of a valid marriage under Muslim Law :-

(1) Proposal and Acceptance : There should first be a proposal made by or on behalf of one of the contracting parties and it must be accepted by the other party or somebody on his behalf. No particular form is necessary but it must be made by the words at one meeting. Under the Sunni (Hanafi) Law, this contract must be made before two male or one male and two female witnesses. But the Shia law does not require the presence of the witnesses.

(2) Consent : A marriage without consent of the parties is invalid. The consent must be of the male and the female who are to be married. The girl who has not attained the age of puberty, the consent of the guardian is essential.

(3) Capacity to Contract : The parties to the marriage should be competent to contract. If they are not competent to contract a valid marriage the contract of marriage should be entered into by their guardians. The capacity to contract means that the parties should be of sound mind, adult and able to give free consent.

(4) No legal disability : The parties to be married must not be within prohibited degrees or so related to each other as to make the union unlawful. The Muslim Law prohibits the marriage among consanguinity, affinity or fosterage.

Formalities of a valid marriage : Marriage may be constituted without any ceremonial; there are no special rites, no officiants, no irksome formalities. Nevertheless, following conditions are necessary:

(a) Offer on the part of one party to the marriage.

(b) Acceptance by the other party

(c) Presence of two witnesses where the parties are Hanafis; no witnesses are required if parties are Shia.

(d) The words with which the marriage is contracted must be clear and unambiguous.

(e) The proposal and acceptance must both be expressed in one and the same meeting.

The offer and acceptance may be made by the parties, or by their agents, if both are competent. In case of legal incompetency, like minority or unsoundness of mind, the guardians may validly enter into a contract of marriage on behalf of their wards.

Legal Effects of a valid Marriage : Baillie gives a description of the legal effects of marriage, but the systematic treatment of this point by Fyzee has been adopted here for convenience.

The following are Nine Legal effects flowing from a valid marriage:

(1) Sexual intercourse becomes lawful and the children born of the union are legitimate;

(2) The wife becomes entitled to maintenance;

(3) The wife becomes entitled to her dower;

(4) The husband becomes entitled to restrain the wife's movements in a reasonable manner;

(5) Mutual rights of inheritance are established;

(6) The prohibitions regarding marriage due to the rules of affinity come into operation;

(7) The wife is not entitled to re-marry after the death of her husband or after the dissolution of her marriage without observing Iddat;

(8) Where there is an agreement between the parties, entered into either at the time of the marriage or subsequent to it, its stipulations will be enforced, in so far as they are consistent with the provisions or the policy of the law; and

(9) Neither the husband nor the wife acquires any interest in the property of the other by reason of marriage.

Question No. 8

Write a short note on Valid, Void and Irregular Marriage ?

Answer :

Muslims are divided into two sects- Shia and Sunni. On the basis of the validity of a marriage, Sunni law classifies a Muslim marriage into the following kinds:

(a) Sahih (valid marriage),

(b) Batil (void marriage) and

(c) Fasid (irregular or invalid marriage).

However, Shia law does not recognize irregular marriage and treats marriages to be either void or valid.

Valid marriage (Sahih)-

A marriage which fulfils all the prescribed conditions of a valid marriage, is considered to be valid. A valid marriage gives rise to the following legal implications:

- The parties acquire the status of husband and wife due to which sexual intercourse between them becomes legal.
- Parties acquire mutual rights of inheritance.
- The wife gets the right of maintenance and right to live with her husband.

- The wife also gets the right of receiving Dower or Mahr from her husband. "Dower" is the sum of money or other property which a Muslim wife gets entitled to receive from her husband in consideration of the marriage.

- The wife is under the obligation to be faithful and obedient to her husband and admit herself to sexual intercourse with him at reasonable time and places.

- The marriage establishes prohibition of marriage due to affinity on both sides, for instance, the husband cannot marry the wife's sister.

- The husband gets the power of reasonable chastisement (punishment) and correction against the wife if she is disobedient or rebellious.

- The husband acquires the right to restrict the wife's movement for valid reasons.

- The children born out of a Sahih marriage are considered to be legitimate.

- On the dissolution of marriage due to death or divorce, the wife is under obligation to perform Iddat. Iddat is the period during which a Muslim woman is prohibited from marrying again after the dissolution of her first marriage. The object of Iddat is to ascertain pregnancy of the wife so as to avoid confusion of parentage.

Void marriage (Batil)

A marriage performed in violation of prescribed legal conditions is called a Batil or void marriage. It is considered void-ab-initio *i.e.* void from its inception and does not create any legal rights and obligations on the parties. It is of no legal effect before or after consummation.

The wife is not entitled to claim maintenance but can claim Dower if the marriage has been consummated. The children born out of a void marriage are considered to be illegitimate.

In case of a void marriage, the parties are free to separate from each other at any time without obtaining a divorce and may contract another marriage lawfully. Following are some instances of a void marriage under Shia law:

- marriage in violation of absolute incapacity.
- marriage with the wife of another person where the marriage is still subsisting.
- remarrying one's own divorced wife if a legal bar exists.
- marriage prohibited by reason of unlawful conjunction.
- marriage with a fifth wife.
- marriage during the pilgrimage.
- marriage with any non-Muslim.
- marriage with a woman undergoing Iddat.

Irregular marriage (Fasid)

A marriage in violation of partial or qualified legal impediments is considered to be an irregular marriage. Marriages which are considered as irregular under Sunni law are void under Shia law. An irregular marriage is not considered to be void from its inception but can be cured by removing the impediments or irregularities, for instance, marriage of a Sunni male with a fire worshiper is irregular which can be made valid by the wife's conversion to Islam.

Muta Marriage

While marriage under Muslim law is mainly classified based on its validity, the Shia law recognizes another kind of marriage called Muta marriage.

The word Muta means "enjoyment". Muta marriage is a temporary marriage with a woman for a fixed period for the purpose of pleasure. Muta marriage is void under Sunni law which treats marriage to be a permanent union. The fixed period of a Muta marriage may be a day, month, year or a term of years.

A male Shia Muslim may contract Muta marriage with a Muslim, Christian or Jewish woman or with a woman who is a fire-worshipper but not with a woman following any other religion. However, a Shia woman cannot contract Muta marriage with a non-Muslim.

For a Muta marriage to be considered as valid, there are 2 conditions--

(a) the period of cohabitation should be fixed and

(b) the Dower should be fixed.

Question No. 9

Define Dower (Mahr). Explain its object and discuss various kinds of Dower ?

Answer :

Mahr or Dower is a sum of money or other property to be paid or delivered to the wife. It is either specified or unspecified but in either case, the law confers a mandatory right of Mahr or Dower on wife.

The Mahr (Dower) belongs to wife and she can deal with it in the manner she likes it and neither her husband nor husband's relations nor even her relations can dictate her in matter of using the Mahr money or property

Definitions of Dower

(1) Mulla : Dower is a sum of money or other property which the wife is entitled to receive from the husband in consideration of the marriage.

(2) Ameer Ali : Dower is a consideration which belongs absolutely to the wife.

(3) Wilson : Dower is a consideration for the surrender of person by the wife. It is technical Anglo-Mohammaden term for its equivalent 'Mahr' in Arabic.

(4) Tyabji : Dower or Mehr is a sum that becomes payable by the husband to the wife on marriage, either by agreement between the parties, or by operation of law.

Object of Dower : The marriage in Muslim Law is a contract. At the time of marriage the bridegroom promises to give certain amount as dower. The dower has the following Four objects:

(1) It is an obligation imposed by the law on the husband as a mark of respect for the wife.

(2) The dower prevents the divorce. The Muslim husband has to pay the entire dower to the wife if he wants to divorce his wife.

(3) The dower amount becomes a strong support to the Muslim Wife, in case, the husband divorces her. She may not suffer in future for her maintenance, if she is divorced.

(4) The dower is a unique feature found in Muslim Law. The dower property of a Muslim Woman cannot be touched by any one. It is fully intact.

Types of Dower

Broadly speaking, there are two kinds of dower.

(a) Specified Dower, and

(b) Unspecified Dower.

But the specified dower has been further divided into :

(1) Prompt Dower, and

(2) Deferred Dower.

(A) Specified Dower :

At the time of marriage or before the marriage if the amount is fixed and agreed between the parties, it is called "Specified Dower". The husband is bound to pay the amount of the Specified Dower.

(1) Prompt Dower : The following are the important points on Promp Dower :-

A. The wife can realise the prompt dower from the husband at any time before or after the consumation.

B. The wife can refuse to enter into conjugal to her husband until her prompt dower is paid.

C. The wife can bring a suit for the recovery of the prompt dower

D. If the wife is minor, the guardian of the bride, can refuse to send her for consumation of the marriage, until the husband pays the prompt dower the amount to her on demand.

E. Limitation : If the wife does not demand the prompt dower, during the period of marriage, the Limitation period starts from the day of the death of the husband or from the day of the dissolution of the marriage.

(2) Defered Dower : The deferred dower shall be payable to the wife on dissolution of marriage by divorce or by death of the husband.

The following are the important points on Deferred Dower :

A. The right of the deferred dower is not a contingent one. It is a vested right of the Muslim wife.

B. If the wife with her free consent wishes to decrease the amount of deferred dower, she can do so.

C. Not only a Muslim wife is entitled to claim the deferred dower but also her heirs entitled to claim the deferred dower after her death.

D. The wife has no right to convert the deferred dower to prompt dower. But the husband, if he wants, can convert it to prompt dower and can pay the dower or transfer any of his property in lieu of the amount.

E. Generally, the deferred dower shall be paid after the dissolution of marriage or after the death of the husband or wife. if any agreement betwe en husband and wife to pay the deferred dower at any time is also valid one.

(B) Unspecified Dower : In such cases where dower has not been settled at the time of the marriage or after, it is fixed with reference to the social position of the wife's family and her own personal qualifications. Help would be taken by taking into consideration the amounts of dower fixed in case of wife's sisters, paternal aunts, etc., such dowers are also called customary dower or proper dower or *Mah-ul-Misl.*

Question No. 10

Distinguish between Prompt Dower & Deferred Dower ?

Answer :

The following are the main differences between prompt dower and deferred dower :

Prompt Dower	Deferred Dower
1. Prompt dower shall be payable immediately after marriage on demand even before the marriage also.	1. It shall be payable on dissolution of marriage by death or divorce.
2. Wife, generally, claims only the prompt dower. It is in the rarest cases, the heirs of the wife claim the prompt dower.	2. The wife, generally, and her heirs also can claim deferred dower.
3. The prompt dower does not become the deferred dower after consummation of marriage and the wife has a right to sue the husband for the recovery of the prompt dower.	3. If the husband wishes, he can convert the deferred dower into prompt dower and pay it to his wife in the shape of cash or property.
4. Generally, when once the prompt dower is fixed, it cannot be decreased.	4. The wife can decrease the deferred dower. The decision must be taken voluntarily.
5. The prompt dower can be demanded by the wife or by his guardian in case of she is minor.	5. The deferred dower can be claimed by the wife or by his heirs.

———————

Question No. 11

State the consequences of non-payment of Dower amount ?

Answer :

The right to dower is an inherent right of every Muslim wife. But, unless this right is effectively enforced, it is of no use to her. Under Muslim law, following means of enforcement of the right to dower are available to a wife (or widow):

Following are the consequences of non-payment of dower amount.

(1) Suit for Dower : The wife or her heirs can bring a suit for the recovery of the dower amount.

(2) Remission of Dower by wife : On demand, the dower must be paid to the wife by her husband or his heirs. If they are unable to pay the dower amount, which is high to their standards, the wife may committee her dower. But the commutation must be made with her own Will and pleasure. No compulsion shall be made against her.

(3) Dower is an Unsecured Debt :—It is unanimously agreed by Muslim jurisprudents that the dower is a debt, but an unsecured debt. She has only right of retention. She is not entitled to any charge on her husband's property.

(4) Limitation : The period of limitation for a suit to recover prompt dower is 3 years from the date on which the dower is demanded and refused. The period of limitation for a suit to recover prompt dower is 3 years from the date of dissolution of the marriage or from the date of death of the husband, or from the date of death of the wife (in case her heirs claim after her death).

(5) Widow As An Her : The widow as an heir is entitled her rights to inherit the property of her husband Alongwith other heirs. She can utilise her rights, as other heirs utilise.

(6) Effect of Conversion : If the Muslim husband converts religion from Islam to any other religion and tries to evade the dower to his wife, even then the wife is entitled to recover her dower.

Section 5 of the Dissolution of Muslim Marriage Act, 1939 entitles a Muslim woman to get her dower amount even on her husband's giving the talaq or her husband's conversion to other religion.

CASES

Nasra Begam vs. Rizwan Ali, (AIR 1980 All 119).

The Allahabad High Court held that the right to dower comes into existence before cohabitation and Prompt Dower may be demanded even before the cohabitation.

Where the wife is minor or insane, her guardian can refuse to allow the husband to take his wife with him till the Prompt Dower has been paid. If the minor wife is already in the custody of her husband, such guardian can take her back on the ground of non-payment of Prompt Dower.

But, where the consummation has taken place even once, the wife's right to refuse consummation is lost. If the marriage has already been consummated, the husband's suit for restitution of conjugal right will not fail on the ground of non-payment of Prompt Dower.

However, the court has discretion, even in such a case, to pass a decree for restitution of conjugal rights subject to the condition of payment of Prompt Dower.

Anis Begum vs. Muhammad Istafa Wali Khan, (AIR 1933 All 634).

The facts were that in the marriage of Anis Begum and Md. Istafa, the Prompt Dower was Rs. 15,000. The husband and wife lived together for some time and a daughter was born to them. Later on, Anis Begum left the house of her husband and refused to come back till her Prompt Dower was satisfied. Md. Istafa, the husband, filed a suit for the restitution of conjugal rights. It was held by Sulaiman, C.J., that there was no absolute right in a husband to claim conjugal rights unconditionally. The courts have discretion to make the decree of restitution of conjugal rights conditional on payment of wife's unpaid Prompt Dower even where the marriage has already been consummated. Accordingly, the decree for restitution of conjugal right was passed in favour of the husband subject to his payment of Rs, 15,000/-.

Question No. 12

What is the difference between Sunni and Shia Law of Dower ?

Answer :

Sunni Law	Shia Law
1. A minimum limit of 10 dirhams (silver coin weighing 2.97 grammes) is prescribed for specified dower.	No minimum limit is prescribede.
2. There is no such maximum limit for proper dower in Sunni law.	Proper dower shall not exceed 500 dirhams. Fixing of dower exceeding 500 dirhams is considered to be abominable though not illegal.
3. If dower is left to be fixed later by the wife, she cannot fix in higher than proper dower and if left to the husband, he cannot fix it lower than proper dower. If it is left to a third person, proper dower would be payable.	If the dower is left be fixed later by the wife, she cannot fix it higher than 500 dirhams and if left to the husband, he may fix any amount.
4. If there is no agreement, showing that what portion is prompt and what portionis deferred,	If there is no agreement showing that what portion is prompt and what portion is deferred, then in Shia law,

then in Sunni law, a reasonable portion of the dower is treated to be prompt dower. Generally half of the dower is treated as deferred dowr.	the whole dower shall be treated as 'prompt dower'.
5. An agreement that no dower shall be due is void.	Such agreement by sane and adult wife is valid.
6. In the absence of an agreement only a reasonable part of the dower is presumed to be prompt.	The whole is presumed to be prompt.
7. Reciprocal marriages are valid and proper dowr becomes payable to each wife	Reciprocal marriages are void but become valid by consummation and proper dower becomes payable.
8. The subject of dower must be in existence.	Usufruct of property not in existence and contingent profits may be subject of dower.
9. If marriage is dissolved by death and dower has not been specified, or it is agreed that no dower shall be payable, proper dower would be due whether the marriage was consummated or not.	If the marriage dissolve by death and dower has not been specified, or it is agreed, that no dower shall be payable, no dower would be due if the marriage was unconsummated.

UNIT -- II

DIVORCE

Question No. 13

What are the different modes in which marriage may be dissolved under Muslim Law ?

Answer :

The marriage in Islam may be dissolved in any one of the following ways :

(a) By the Death of spouse;

(b) By the Act of the parties; and

(c) By the Judicial process.

(a) By the Death of Spouse : It is clear that with the death of husband or wife the marriage tie comes to an end. When the wife dies, the husband may remarry immediately, but in case of husband's death, widow has to wait till the expiry of IDDAT (4 months and 10 days or if pregnant till delivery).

(b) By the Act of the Parties : The marriage can dissolve by the Act of any one of the parties to the marriage. In fact, the Islamic Law has given the absolute power to the husband to give the divorce. The same power is not given to the wife. However, the Dissolution of the Marriage can be done by the act of the parties to the marriage.

(1) By the Act of the Husband ; And

(2) By the Act of the Wife.

(I) By the Act of the Husband

The husband may give divorce to his wife in the following different ways :

(a) Talaq.

(i) Talaq-us-sunnat (*i.e.,* in conformity with the dictates of Prophet)

(ii) Talaq-ul-Biddat (*i.e.,* of innovation, therefore not approved)

(b) ILA (vow of continence)

(c) ZIHAR (Injurious comparison)

(a) Talaq : In literary sense Talaq means repudiation or to repudiate the wife. In another sense this Arabic word means "taking off any tie or restraint". In Hanafi Law, no special form or phrase is necessary to pronounce talak. However, the Shia Law, insist on strict adherence to a form, *i.e.,* it must be in the Arabic languge uttered orally, in the presence uttered orally, the presence and hearing of two male witnesses, who should be honest and virtuous Muslims.

(i) Talaq-Us-Sunnat : It means, a talak which carries the approval of the Prophet. It may be in the most approved form *i.e.,* Ahsan or Hasan *i.e.,* simply a approved form.

Ahsan (Most Approved) : Hedaya brands it as the most laudable divorce where the husband repudiates his wife by a single pronouncement in a period of Tuhr (purity, *i.e.,* when the wife is free from her menstrual courses), during which he has not had intercourse with her and then leaves her to the observance of Iddat. The divorce remains revocable during the Iddat and the parties retain the right of inheritance.

According to Hedaya, this method of divorce is the most approved because the companions of the Prophet approved of it, because it remains within the power of the husband to revoke the divorce during Iddat which is 3 months or till delivery in case of pregnancy.

Hasan (Approved) : It is also an approved form but less approved than the Ahsan. The husband successively pronounces divorce three times during consecutive periods of Tuhr (purity). It is, therefore, "a divorce upon a divorce", where the first and second pronouncements are revoked and followed by a third, only then Talaq becomes irrevocable. It is essential that no intercourse should have taken place during that particular period of purity in which the pronouncement has been made.

(ii) Talaq-Ul-Biddat : Here the husband does not follow the approved form of Talaq *i.e.,* Talaq-us-Sunnat, and neither pays any attention to the period of purity nor to the abstention from intercourse.

Talaq-ul-Bidat consists of : (1) Triple Divorce *i.e.,* three pronouncements made during a sing Tuhr (purity) either in one sentence, *e.g.,* "I divorce you Thrice" or in separate sentences.

(2) One irrevocable Divorce :—A single pronouncement made during a Tuhr (purity) clearly indicating an intention irrevocably to dissolve the marriage *e.g.,* "I divorce you irrevocably".

(3) The Muslim has given an absolute power to the Muslim husband to divorce his wife at any time without showing any cause, even in the intoxication or under compulsion, force etc. Further, the Islamic Law also has given the Muslim

husband the "Delegation of power to divorce". It means, the husband may delegate his power to divorce to any other third person or to his wife. In such a case, the wife may utilise to take divorce by pronouncing the Talak-Ahsan or Talaq Hasan whichever she adopts. Likewise the third person, who is delegated may pronounce the divorce.

In *Shayara Bano vs. Union of India and others*, AIR 2017 SC 4609, the Hon'ble Supreme Court of India declared the practice of triple talaq to be unconstitutional being in violation of Article 14 of the Constitution of India. Act banning Talaq-ul-Biddat has been passed in the Parliament.

(4) The Sunni school recognised the talak under compulsion or under the influence of intoxication by the husband. The Shia school does not recognise such type of talak.

(5) Hanafi (Sunni) Law, as distinguished from the Shia Law, holds a divorce pronounced in fest (joke, fun, etc.) as valid according to Hedaya.

(b) ILA (Vow of Continence) : In ILA, when the husband swears that he will not have sexual inter course with his wife, and abstains from it for four months (4 months) or more the divorce is effected. He may revoke the oath by resumption of marital life within the time for which he swears. After the expiry of the period of four months, the marriage is dissolved without legal process in Hanafi (Sunni) Law. But under shia law, the legal proceedings are necessary. This form is unknown to India.

(c) Zihar (Injurious Comparison) : If the husband compares his wife to his mother or any other female within prohibited degrees, the wife has a right to refuse to cohabit with him until he has performed penance. If the husband refuses to express his penance, then the wife may apply for a judicial process i.e. Divorce. This mode of Talak is very rare in India.

(ii) By the Act of the wife : The husband may delegate the power of divorce to his wife. He may do so at the time of marriage contract or at any time when he so likes. In fact, the Islamic Law has given an absolute power to the husband to divorce his wife at any time without showing any cause. In this particular type of divorce, the wife can obtain the divorce from her husband in the following manner :

(a) Delegated power of her husband

(b) Khula (Redemption)

(c) Mubara'a (Mutual Freeing)

(a) Delegated Power of Her Husband : When dispute arises between husband and wife, the husband becomes angry and annoyed and says his wife to divorce and gives the authority to his wife to take the divorce whenever she likes before two witnesses by any are of the modes of Talak Ahsan or Talak Hasan, whichever, she likes.

(b) Khula (Redemption) : If the mutual relationship between the husband and wife is not good, the wife if she so desires, may seek a Khula divorce, *e.g.,* by relinquishing her claim to the dower. However, it entirely depends upon the husband to accept the consideration of dower and to grant the divorce. Khula may be for any consideration - Dower, money or property, etc.

The leading case a *Khula divorce is Munshee Buzul-Raheem vs. Lateefunnissa,* (1861) 8 MIA 379, in which it was observed that a divorce by Khula is at once complete from the moment when the husband repudiates the wife. There is no period during which such a divorce can be repudiated.

(c) Mubara'a (Mutual Freeing) : When the is divorce is effected by mutual consent of the husband and wife, it is known as mubara'a *i.e.*, freeing one another mutually. In Khula, the offer comes from the wife, but in Mubara'a, the offer may come from wife or husband. Once the offer of one spouse is accepted by the husband the divorce operates as a single irrevocable divorce.

In the above mentioned three types of divorces, the wife has to observe the period of Iddat, and she is entitled to maintenance.

C. Judicial Process :

(1) Lian (Mutual Imprecation) : The wife is entitled to sue for a divorce on the ground that her husband has falsely charged her with adultery. At the hearing of the suit, the husband had two alternatives :

(a) He may withdraw the charge before the end of the trial, in which case the wife could not get a divorce.

or

(b) to persist in his attitude, whereby he will be required to accuse his wife on oath. This is followed by oaths of innocence made by the wife. After these "mutual imprecations", the court dissolves the marriage.

(2) Faskh (Judicial Annulment) : Faskh means annulment. It refers to the power of Kazi (in India, Law Court) to annual a marriage on the application of the wife. The law of Faskh is founded upon Koran and Traditions (Sunna).

According to Bukhari, "If a woman be prejudiced by a marriage, let it be broken off".

In India, such judicial annulments are governed by Section 2 of the Dissolution of Muslim Marriages Act, 1939. It lays down the following grounds on which wife can seek divorce :

(1) Where about the husband have not been known for a period of 4 years;

(2) Neglect of husband to provide for wife's maintenance for a period of 2 years ;

(3) Imprisonment of husband for seven (7) years or more ;

(4) Failure to perform marital obligations for 3 years;

(5) Impotency of husband

(6) Insanity for a period of 2 years, or leprosy or a virulent veneral disease;

(7) Repudiation of marriage by wife before she attains the age of 18 years, if she was married by her father or other guardian before she was 15 years, provided marriage is not consummated;

(8) Husband's forcing her to lead immoral life, or disposing of her property or making hindrances in her religious practices, etc., *i.e.*, treats her with cruelty.

(9) Any other ground recognized by Muslim Law.

Question No. 14

What are the Legal effects of divorce under Muslim Law ?

Answer :

The following are the Legal effects of divorce

(1) Cohabitation becomes illegal : Cohabitation between the husband and wife becomes unlawful after completion of the divorce.

(2) Iddat : The wife is required to observe an Iddat of three lunar months after the divorce or, if pregnant, till the delivery of the child. However, if the divorce takes place before consummation, the wife need not observe Iddat.

(3) Maintenance during Iddat : During the period of Iddat, the divorced wife is entitled to be maintained by her former husband. Maintenance of divorced wife is now governed by the Muslim Women (Protection of Rights on Divorce) Act, 1986. Under this Act to the former husband is liable to maintain the divorced wife only upto the period of Iddat.

(4) Right to Contract another Marriage : Both the parties are free to contract another marriage with other persons. Thus, husband can marry another woman immediately after the divorce. But a divorced wife cannot marry another husband before the expiry of the period of Iddat. If their marriage had dissolved before the consummation, the wife is also free to contract another marriage immediately after the divorce.

(5) Dower : The unpaid dower becomes immediately payable to the divorced wife. Whether the dower is prompt or Deferred, the divorced wife is entitled to it immediately after the divorce.

(6) Remarriage between the Divorced Couple : After completion of divorce, the parties cease to be husband and wife. There is no restriction in their re-marriage with other persons.

(7) Mutual Rights of Inheritance Ceases : Upon the completion of a divorce *i.e.* when it becomes irrevocable, the mutual rights of inheritance between the spouses cease. That is to say, if husband dies after the divorce, the wife is not entitled to inherit his properties. In the same manner, if the wife dies, the husband cannot inherit her properties. But, if the divorce was pronounced during the husband's death-illness (Marz-ul-Maut), this general rule is not applicable.

Question No. 15

Write a key note on 'Apostacy and conversion as grounds of Divorce ?

Answer :

When a Muslim renounces or leaves Islam it is called "Apostacy", whereas when a Non-Muslim embraces or accepts Islam, it is known as "conversion".

Apostacy and conversion may affect the marriage the in the following circumstances.

Apostacy :

(a) Where Husband renounces Islam.

(b) Where Wife renounces Islam

Conversion :

(c) Where Husband embraces Islam.

(d) Where Wife embraces Islam

(a) Where husband renounces Islam : Where a Muslim husband renounces Islam, his marriage with his Muslim wife is dissolved *ipso facto*.

As to what constitutes an act "Act of apostacy", the Lahore High Court in *Resham Bibi vs. Khudo Baksh* (1937) Lah. 277, held that a formal declaration is sufficient *e.g.* "I hereby renounce Islam".

(b) Where Wife Renounces Islam : Section 4 of the Dissolution of Muslim Marriages Act - 1939 says that "The renunciation of Islam by a married Muslim woman shall not by itself operate to dissolve her marriage.

(c) Where Husband Embraces Islam : According to Ameer Ali, if a Christian or Jew (or anybody else following a Divine Book) embraces Islam, his marriage with his Christian or Jewish wife is not dissolved. It will be dissolved, however, if the wife belongs to a non-scriptural religion (*i.e.,* Hinduism or Buddhism or Jainism etc.) because of the fact that a Muslim cannot marry are non-kitabia woman. Islam has to be offered to such a wife, if she refuses to embrace it, divorce may be given. This offer shall be made by the husband and law court has nothing to do with it.

(d) Where wife embraces Islam : If a non-Muslim wife, whether she is a Christian, Jew, Irani Zorastrian or Hindu embraces Islam, her marriage tie stands intact, irrespective of the fact that the husband is non-Muslim.

For instance, it was held by the Calcutta High Court in *Noor Jehan vs. Eugene Tischenko,* (1942) 2 Cal. 165, that the marriage of a Christian (Russian) wife with her Christian husband is not dissolved merely because the wife has accepted the Islam.

Similarly, the Bombay High Court has observed in the case of *Robaba Khannum vs. Khodadad Bomanji Irani* where Robaba, a Zoroastrian wife, embraced Islam but her husband did not embrace the Islam.

Question No. 16

Define Iddat. Explain its object and effects ?

Answer :

Definitions given by the different authors are given below :

(1) Asaf A. A. Fyzee : When a marriage is dissolved by by death or divorce, the woman is prohibited from marrying within a specified time. This period is called "Iddat".

(2) Ameer Ali : Iddat is an interval which the woman is bound to observe between the termination, by death or divorce of one matrimonial alliance and commencement of another.

Object : It is the period of continence imposed on a woman on the termination of a marriage in the interests of certainty of paternity during which a woman is supposed to live a life of seclusion and to abstain from certain luxuries.

Effects of Iddat : (1) During the period of Iddat, the wife is entitled to maintenance.

(2) During the period of Iddat, the wife is not entitled to marry another person.

(3) The wife is entitled to deferred dower. If the prompt dower is not paid, it must immediately be paid.

(4) Where the husband pronounces Talak three times during death-illness and dies before completion of wife's iddat, the wife is entitled to inherit from him even if the divorce has become irrevocable prior to his death.

(5) During the period of iddat, if any one of the party to the marriage, dies, the other is entitled to inherit from him or

her in his or her capacity of wife or husband respectively as the case may be, if the divorce has not become irrevocable before the death of the deceased.

Duration of Iddat

(1) Iddat of Widowhood : When the husband dies, the wife is prohibited to marry another person for a period of 4 months 10 days, from the date of death of her husband.

(2) Iddat of Talk : Where the divorce takes place, the duration of the iddat is 3 menstruation periods, or 3 lunar months. If the woman is pregnant at the time of the divorce, the iddat period continues until the delivery.

(3) Iddat of Pregnant Woman : Where the wife is pregnant at the time of the time of the death of her husband, the iddat period continues until the delivery. If delivery or its miscarriage comes before 4 months and 10 days, the remaining period will have to be observed.

(4) Consumation of Marriage : If the marriage is not consumated, iddat is to be observed in the case of death of the husband from the death of the husband. In the case of divorce, it is not necessary to observe the iddat period.

(5) Divorce and Death : Where a husband divorces his wife, from the date of divorce the iddat period starts.

(6) Irregular marriage : In certain circumstances, the marriage takes place during the period of iddat, such marriage is declared irregular (in case of sunni) or void (in the case of shia). If the wife and husband do not cohabit, the wife need not observe the iddat. If the marriage consumated, she has to observe the iddat.

Question No. 17

Who are the persons entitled to maintenance under Muslim Law and explain the basis and extent of Liability ?

Answer :

According to Muslim Law, a Muslim is bound to provide maintenance (Nafqa) to the following persons. They are :

1. Wife.

2. Aged Parents.

3. Children and Grand-children.

4. Other relatives, Servants.

1. Wife :—It is the duty of husband to maintain his wife whether she be Muslim or Kitabiah (follower of spiritual book), poor or rich, young or old. It is the duty of the wife to be faithful to his husband. The husband need not maintain his wife is he is not loyal to him and wilfully resides with her parents or neglects him or disobedience to her husband.

If the husband has not paid the prompt dower or she refuses to live with her husband because of his cruelty, the husband is bound to maintain her. It was held by the Allahabad High Court in *Badruddin vs. Aisha Begum,* (1957) that where has married a second wife or keeps a mistress, the wife may refuse to live with the husband and still claim maintenance from him.

The Muslim husband, if agrees the provisions of Section 125 Code of Criminal Procedure in the case of a maintenance by his wife, then only he provisions of Section 125 Code of

Criminal Procedure will apply to him otherwise it will not apply to him.

2. Aged Parents :--It is a pious obligation of every Muslim to maintain his aged parents, who are unable to maintain themselves and have no means for their livelihood.

A Muslim is bound to maintain his paternal and maternal grandfathers and grandmothers, if they are poor, and are unable to maintain themselves, and have no means for their livelihood. Provision of Section 125 Code of Criminal Procedure will apply in case of aged parents.

3. Children and Grandchildren :--In case of maintenance, the child is entitled to get maintenance until the age of 18 years (not the age of puberty. The Doctrine of age of puberty (Majority) applies in Muslim Law in matters of marriage, dower and divorce only. In other subject, the provisions of the Indian Majority Act, 1875 shall apply.

2. Every father is bound to maintain his children, until they attain the age of majority. He is also bound to maintain his major children, who are disabled by infirmity or decease.

3. In Muslim Law, the Muslim is bound to maintain his minor daughter until her marriage. If the child is under the custody of mother, then also the father is bound to maintain the child.

4. Step-mother and step-father is not bound to maintain the child.

5. In case the father has no property, and has no means to provide maintenance to his children or by any reason of disease and at the same time, the mother has the income source or property to meet the maintenance, then she has to

maintain the children. In other words, mother steps into the shoes of the father.

6. Under Muslim Law, the father is not bound to maintain his illegitimate child.

4. Other relatives :--All persons who are in "easy circumstances" are bound to maintain their poor relations who are withnthe prohibited degrees by consanguinity in propertion to the shares which they would iherit at the time of the death of such poor relations.

Question No. 18

Explain about Muslim Women (Protection of Rights on Divorce) Act, 25 of 1986 ?

Answer :

Law Before 1986 : Section 125 of Code of Criminal Procedure was in force regarding the maintenance of Muslim Woman equally with Hindu woman. Section 125 Code of Criminal Procedure provides that the husband is bound to provide maintenance to his wife, children (Legal or illegal) and also old aged parents. The famous leading case law interpreted that the section gives the Muslim Woman to get the maintenance from her husband even after divorce, and if she does not re-marry, and who is unable to maintain herself.

CASE LAW

Shah Bano's Case (1986). *Mohammed Ahmed Khan vs. Shah Bano Begum,* AIR 1985 SC 945 and also 1985 Cr.LJ. 875.

In this case, the court granted the maintenance to the wife, even after the divorce, so long as she has not remarried.

This case caused a sensational agitation among the Muslim community throughout the country. The entire Muslim community felt that by the Supreme Court's decision which granted the maintenance to the wife (Mrs. Shah Bano Begum) even after the divorce as per Section 125 of Code of Criminal Procedure. Which overrides the Muslim Personal Law and it was direct interference of the court in the Muslim Personal Law. Thus, a great controversy arose. In order to satisfy the Muslims (who are the second largest community in the country), the then Prime Minister, Rajiv Gandhi, made an

Act *i.e.*, The Muslim Woman (Protection of Rights on Divorce) Act of 1986.

Law After The Act of 1986 : Section 5 of the Act of 1986 provides that if both the

husband and wife give their consent admitting the Section 125 of Code of Criminal Procedure through an affidavit, then the concerned Magistrate / Judge shall dispose of the case according to Section 125 of Code of Criminal Procedure. Generally, no husband gives his consent for the trial under Section 125 Code of Criminal Procedure which burdens more liability upon him. While his personal law permits to pay the maintenance only for a period of Iddat only.

After the Act of 1986, the Muslim husband is not bound to maintain his wife after divorce. He has to pay maintenance for a period of Iddat only. Thereafter, no liability lies upon him.

Main Features of the Act 25 OF 1986

1. This Act has passed in the month of May 1986 by the Rajiv Gandhi's Government in order to pacific the Muslim Community aggrieved by the decision of Shah Bano's case of Supreme Court.

2. There are seven sections in this Act.

3. The Muslim husband has the liability to maintain the Muslim wife until the period of Iddat only from the date of divorce. If she is pregnant at the time of divorce, then till the delivery of a child. After the completion of the period of Iddat or delivery of a child, it ceases automatically.

4. The liability of maintenance of a divorced wife shifts from the husband to her relatives. If the relative refuse to maintain her, she may bring the suit for maintenance against them.

5. The Muslim husband, if a agrees, the provisions of Section 125 of Code of Criminal Procedure in the case of maintenance by his wife, then only the provisions of Section 125 Will apply to him.

6. The consent of the husband must be expressed by an affidavit or any other, such form as may be prescribed, but it must be in writing.

7. The declaration of the consent may be joint or separate. It is purely an option. It depends upon the husband whether to opt Section 125 Code of Criminal Procedure or not. If he does not opt, the court will not compel him to opt it, but if once accepted it cannot be revoked.

Question No. 19

What is the difference between Shia Law and Sunni Law Relating to Maintenance ?

Answer :

Shia Law	Sunni Law
1. It is not obligatory to maintain the father if he is able to earn.	1. It is obligatory to maintain even if the father is able to earn himself.
2. In case there are more persons than one who are liable to maintain, the burden is shared according to the means and ability of each.	2. In case there are more persons than one who are liable to maintain, the liability of maintenance is shared equally.
3. When the father is poor and the mother rich, the liability to maintain the infant children in such circumstances rests primarily on the grand father, if he has means, and not on the mother even thugh she be rich.	3. When the father is poor and the mother rich, the liability to maintain the infant children falls on the mother even though the children may have a rich paternal grand father.
4. The wife is entitled to past maintenance even in the absence of an agreement to that effect.	4. The wife is not entitled to past maintenance except when there is distinct agreement.

5. The Collaterals are not liable for maintenance. There is obligation only to maintain descendants and ascendants namely, sister, brother, uncle or aunt, whether maternal or paternal.	5. Muslims having means are bound to maintain their poor relatives within the prohibited degrees in the same proportions in which they would inherit from such collaterials.
6. The amount of maintenance of the wife according to wife's requirements in respect of conditions, clothes, food, residence anointing and as also the customs of her equals among her own people in the same city.	6. In fixing the amount of maintenance payable by the husband to the wife the Hanafi law pays regard to the position of both the husband and the wife.
7. Shia law, though considers the entitlement of pregnant divorced wife for maintenance till the delivery iif it takes place beyond the expiry of period of idat.	7. Divorced wife is entitled to maintenance during iddat period only, whether she is pregnant or not.

Question No. 20

What is the Triple Talaq Law ?

Answer :

Talaq is an Islamic word for divorce, denoting dissolution of marriage when a Muslim man can severe all marital ties with his wife. Under the Muslim law, Triple Talaq means liberty from the relationship of marriage, eventually or immediately, where the man, by simply uttering the word 'talaq' three times, ends his marriage. This instant divorce is called Triple Talaq, also known as 'talaq-e-biddat'.

The Muslim Personal Law (Shariat) Application Act of 1937 had legalised and allowed the practice of Triple Talaq which gave a Muslim husband special privileges over his wife.

Triple Talaq Law, also known as Muslim Women (Protection of Rights on Marriage) Act, 2019, was passed by the Indian Parliament, to make instant Triple Talaq a criminal offence.

Triple Talaq void and illegal : According to Clause 3 in Chapter 2, "any pronouncement of talaq by a person upon his wife, by words, either spoken or written or in electronic form or in any other manner whatsoever, shall be void and illegal".

Punishment for pronouncing Triple Talaq : The Clause 3 also states that, "whoever pronounces Triple Talaq upon his wife shall be punished with imprisonment for a term which may extend to three years and fine".

According to Clause 7 (c) in Chapter 3, "No person accused of an offence punishable under Triple Talaq law shall be released on bail after the Magistrate, on an application filed by the accused and after hearing the married Muslim woman upon whom talaq was pronounced, is convinced that there are reasonable grounds for granting bail to the accused".

Custody of children : Clause 6 in Chapter 3 states that, "a married Muslim woman shall be entitled to custody of her minor children in the event of pronouncement of talaq by her husband, in such manner as may be determined by the Magistrate".

Question No. 21

What is the distinction between Dower and Dowry ?

Answer :

Dowry is a very wide term and used in different ommunities and nations in different meanings. The system of dowery existed in almost all ancient civilization and even in the modern Hindu society. In India majority of marriges are settled through negotiations for amount to be paid to the husband bythe parents of bride. As per Section (2) of the Dowry Prohibition Act, 1961, 'dowry' means any property or valuable security given to agreed to be given either directly or indirectly: (a) by one party to a marrige to the other party to the marriage or (b) by the parents of either party to a marriage or by other person to either party to the marriage or to any other person, at or before or any time after the marriage in connection with the marriage of the said parties, but does not include dower or mahr in the case of persons to whom the Muslim Personal Law (Shariat) applies. But dower is the payment by the bridegroom to the bride at the time of marriage among Mohammedans. The following are the differences between dower and dowry.

S.No.	Dower	Dowry
1.	Dower is existed in Muslim community since the pre-Islamic time. It is an old custom and is gien an honour from time immemorial.	Dowry is an evil practice and new custom crept in India, especially in Hindu community.
2.	Dower is paid by the husband to wife either voluntarily or custmarily.	Dowry is demanded from the side of the Bride-groom and his parents.
3.	Dower is the considera-tion for marriage and for the welfare of the Muslim wife.	Dowry is a payment for the status of bridegroom, bargained and squeezed from bride's parents.
4.	Dower prevents the Muslim husband to gie the divorce to his wife.	Dowry system leads for dowry deaths.
5.	Dower is seen only in Muslim community.	Dowry system creepted into all communities in India including Muslim community.
6.	Dower is not punishable.	Giving and taking dowry is punishale.
7.	Dowr is settled between the bridegroomand bride before the marriage and shall be payable before the marriage or after the	Dowry is the payment by the bride's parents tot he bridegroom's parents before the marriage and even after the marriage.

	Dower	Dowry
	marriage, or even after the death of the eithr party to the marriage.	
8.	Dower is an unsecured debt.	It is not a debt but an Evil social custom.
9.	Payment of Dower is legal obligation in Mohammedan law.	Giving and taking of dowry is punishable as per the Dowry Prohibition Act, 1961.
10.	Dower is a mark of respect for the wife.	Dowry is a burden some on the parents of bride.

The Dowry Prohibition Act, 1961 prohibited giving and taking the dowry.

Section 3 of the Act, provides that if any person after the commencement of the Act, gives or takes or abets the giving or taking of dowry, he shall be punishable with imprisonment for a term which shall not be less than five years and with fine which shall not be less than fifteen thousand rupees or the amount of the value of such dowry, which ever is more.

Acdcording Section 4 of the Act, if any person demands, directly or indirectly from the parents or other relaties or guardian of a bride or bridegroom, as the case may be, any dowry he shall be punishable with imprisonment for a term which shall not be less than six months, but which may extend to two years, and with fine which may extend to the thousand rupees.

UNIT -- III

PATERNITY, GIFT AND WILL

Question No. 22

What is meant by Acknowledgement of Paternity or Legitimacy. What are its requirements ?

Answer :

Acknowledgement : Where the paternity of a child cannot be proved by establishing a marriage between his parents as the time of his conception or birth, the Muslim Law recognises such 'acknowledgment' as a method whereby such marriage and legitimate descent can be established as a matter of substantive law for purpose of inheritance.

This doctrine relates only to cases where the fact of a marriage itself or the exact time of its occurrence with reference to the legitimacy of the acknowledged child is not proved. The acknowledgment of paternity may be either exprêss or implied.

Requirements of a Valid Acknowledgment

In order that an acknowledgment must be valid and effective, following conditions/requirements must be fulfilled:

1. The acknowledgment of legitimacy arises only if the paternity of the child is not certain.
2. All illegitimate child cannot be acknowledged as legitimate.

3. The ages of parties must be such as to be in consonance with the presumption of paternity. *E.g.,* A father aged 30 years cannot acknowledge a son aged 22 years. Acknowledge must be 12 years older than the acknowledged.

4. The child acknowledged must not be known to be the child of another man.

5. Person acknowledged must not be offspring of Zina.

6. The acknowledgement must not have been repudiated by the person acknowledged.

7. The acknowledgment must be adult and same. He must possess the legal capacity for entering into a valid contract.

8. Once a valid acknowledgment of paternity is made, it cannot be revoked by the father.

9. The acknowledgement must be not merely of sonship, but of legitimate sonship.

10. The acknowledgement must be with the distinct intention of conferring the status of legitimacy.

The observations of the Allahabad High Court on acknowledgement of paternity in *Muhammad Allahabad vs. Muhammad Ismail,* (1888-10- All. 289) are relevant. In that case, the Court observed :

"The Muhammadan law of acknowledgement of parentage, with its legitimating effect, has no reference whatsoever to cases in which the illegitimacy of the child is proved and established, either by reason of a lawful union between the parents of the child being impossible (as in the case of an incestuous intercourse or an adulterous connection), or by reason of a marriage, necessary to render the child legitimate, being disproved.

The doctrine relates only to cases where either the fact of the marriage itself or the exact time of its occurrence with reference to the legitimacy of the acknowledged child is not proved in the sense of law, as distinguished from disproved. In other words, the doctrine applies only to cases of uncertainty as to legitimacy, and in such cases, acknowledgement has its effect, but that effect always proceeds upon the assumption of a lawful union between the parents of the acknowledged child.

Effect of Acknowledgment of Paternity

1. Acknowledgment of child means acknowledgment of wife also.

2. It raises presumption of marriage.

3. It gives rights of inheritance to children, parents and wife.

4. Acknowledgment once made is irrevocable.

Question No. 23

What are the Kinds of Guardians and What are the powers of Legal Guardians ?

Answer :

Muslim Law recognises Three kinds of guardianship namely:

(a) Guardianship of Person.

(b) Guardianship of Property.

(c) Guardianship in Marriage.

(a) Guardianship of Person : Guardianship of the person of the minor belongs to the following in the order they are mentioned below :

(1) Mother : Mother is entitled to the custody (Hizanat) :—

Sunni Law

(a) A male-child till 7 years.

(b) A female-child till puberty, which is either 15 or 18 years.

Shia Law

(a) A male-child till 2 years.

(b) A female-child till 7 years.

In the case of *Imambandi vs. Mustaddi,* (1918) 45 IA 73, it was observed by the Privy Council that under Muslim Law, the mother is entitled only to the custody of the person of her minor child upto a certain age according to the sex of the child. But, she is not the natural guardian, the father alone or if he is dead, his executor (under the sunni law) is the legal guardian.

It is observed by Tyabji that where the husband and wife are living together, the child must stay with them, and the husband cannot take the child away with him; nor can the mother, even during the period that she is entitled to the custody of the child, take it away without the permission of the father.

The father's supervision over the child continues inspite of the child being under the care of female relations, because the burden of providing maintenance to the child rests exclusively on the father. The mother's right of custody is not lost merely by her being divorced. But where she marries a second husband, the custody of children normally belongs to her former husband.

Failing mother and female relations, the following male relations may act as guardian in the order they are mentioned below :

(1) Father

(2) Nearest paternal grandfather

(3) Full brother

(4) Consanguine brother, and other paternal relations within the prohibited degrees.

The custody of a boy over 7 years of age, and of an un-married girl who has attained puberty belongs to :

(1) Father

(2) The Executor appointed byt he father's will.

(3) The father's father how high so ever

(4) The male paternal relations in the same order as for inheritance; and

(5) Failing all the above, it is for the court to appoint a guardian of such minors.

B. Guardianship of Property

The Muslim Law recognises the three types of guardians for the purposes of guardianship of property namely;

(i) Legal Guardians or Dejure Guardian

(ii) Guardians appointed by court or certified guardianship

(iii) Defacto Guardians.

(i) Legal Guardian or De Jure Guardian : The Legal Guardian are also known De-jure Guardian under Hanafi (Sunni) Law, the following are the guardians of minor's property, in order of priority:

(a) Father;

(b) Executor appointed by father's will;

(c) Father's father

(d) Executor appointed by Paternal Grandfather; and

(e) Executor of the last named executor.

Thus, the only persons who are entitled to appoint a guardian of the property of a minor by Will are his father and father's father. The mother has no power to appoint by Will a guardian of the property of her minor child. According to Muslim Law, Mother, brother, uncle, etc. are not legal guardians or De-jure Guardians.

The executor of the father's Will, according to Hanafi (Sunni) Law, has preference over grandfather. In Shia Law, some hold that the father cannot appoint an executor in the presence of a grandfather, who will have preference over father's executor in superintending the property. According to Shafei Law, the grandfather has preferential rights over teh father's executor in matters of property management.

A Legal Guardian (De Jure Guardian) has power to sell or pledge teh goods or chattles of teh minor for the minors imperatienecessatives - such as foods, clothing or nursing.

Generally, Muslim Law does not allow legal guardian to alienate immovable properties of a minor. The following exceptions to this general rule are recognises.

(1) Where the sale may fetch double the value of the property.

(2) Where minor has no other property, and sle is necessary for minor maintenance.

(3) Where there are no other means of paying debts of the deceased,

(4) Where the income is less than the expenses of the proeprty;

(5) Where the property is falling into decay;

(6) Where the property has been usurped (i.e. wrongly fully seized or encroached upon) and the guardians fears taht there is no chance of fair restitution.

(ii) Certified Guardianship : In the absence of legal guardians, the court is competent to appoint guardian for the protection and preservation of minor's property, as it was observed in the case of *Imambandi vs. Mustaddi,* (1918). Such guardian is called as "Certified Guardian" by the Court. A guardian of the property of a minor is appointed by the court under the Guardians and Wards Act, 1890. he cannot alienate immovable property of minor without the permission of the court and without necessary or advantage of the minor. But, he may, with the prior permission of the court, mortgage, sell, gift away or exchange the property, and also lease any, part of that property for a term exceeding 5 years. Any alienation in contravention of the above provisions is voidable at the instance of minor, or any person affected by such any alienation.

(iii) De Facto Guardian : A person, who is neither a legal guardian, nor a guardian appointed by the court, but has voluntarily placed himself in charge of the person and property of the minor, such person is known as De Facto Guardian.

A Defacto Guardian has to same power to sell and pledge the goods and chattles of the minor in his charge as a legal guardian of his property. But he cannot enter into any contract whereby the minor would be saddled with any pecuniary liability.

A De-facto Guardian has no right to alienate immovable property of a minor. Such a transfer is void. Thus a sale, mortgage, or any other transfer by mother who is a De Facto guardian, is absolutely void.

In the case of *Mir Sarwarjan vs. Fakhruddin,* (1912), it was held by the Privy Council that the guardian of minor (whether he be legal, certified or De facto) has no right to make an agreement for the purchase of immovable property on behalf of the minor; a such an agreement is void.

(c) Guardianship in Marriage : The Muslim Jurisprudence permits the marriage between teh minors and such marriage if conducted by the De Jure guardians for the welfare of the minors. Generally this power is given to the father of the child. The guardianship in marriage is called 'Jabar'. The following persons are entitled to act as Guardians in Marriage.

(1) Father

(2) The Father's Father how high so ever

(3) Full brother and other male relations on the Father's side.

(4) Mother

(5) Maternal Relations within prohibited Degrees

(6) The Kazi or the court.

Powers of Legal Guardians : The Legal guardians of the property of a minor have the following powers.

1. As a general rule, the legal guardian is not entitled to alienate the minor's property except in the following circumstances :

(a) For the bare and legal necessities of the minor;

(b) Where the expenses exceed the income of the property;

(c) Where the property may be lost, if not sold within the time;

(d) Where double value than the market value is available on the sale of such property;

(e) Any other reason which the legal guardian opines that the sale or mortgage is compulsory and unavoidable for the welfare of the minor, he may sell such immovable property, etc. etc.

2. A certified guardian appointed by the court must obtain the court's permission for the sale of any immovable property of the minor. It is a mandatory rule.

3. A defacto guardian has no power to alienate any property of the minor of any reason.

4. The legal guardian is not competent to enter into agreement for the purchase of immovable property for the minor. Such agreement is void.

5. A legal guardian of a minor is competent and has power to sell or pledge the movable property of the minor for the welfare and legal necessity of the minor child. But such power must very cautiously be utilised. The paramount consideration must be the welfare of the child.

Question No. 24

What is the differences between Sunni and Shia Law relating to Guardianship ?

Answer :

There is no much difference between Sunni and Shia Law relating guardianship. However these two laws differ relating guardianship as given below.

1. Under Sunni Law, the mother is entitled to the custody of the boy upto seven years, and a girl until she attains puberty, whereas, under Shia Law, the mother is entitled to the custody of boy upto two years and a girl upto seven years.

2. Under the Sunni Law, the lawful guardians of the minor's property are in order of preference : the father, the executor appointed by a will of the father; and after him the guardian appointed by the executor, the father's father; the executor appointed by the father's father, and tghe executor of the last named executor. But, under Shia Law, if the grandfather is alive, he is entitld to the guardianship of the minor's proeprty in preference to tghe father's executors.

3. Under Sunni Law, the order of guardianship for the purpose of marriage is (i) father, (ii) paternal grand father how highsoever, (iii) brother and other remote male paternal relatives in the same order as for him heritance, (iv) the mother, (v) other maternal relations within the prohibited

degrees and failing all these (vi) the Stale But, the Shia Law recognise only father and grandfatehr, howsoever as the guardians of marriage.

Question No. 25

Define Gift (Hiba). What are the essential requirements of a valid Gift under Muslim Law ?

Answer :

In Muslim law, gifts are called "hiba". The gifts in India are governed by Transfer of Property Act, 1872. However, the provision of Transfer of Property Act, 1872 does not apply to Muslim law. The English term, 'gift' is of a wider connotation and applies to all transactions where one transfer's one's property to another without any consideration. The term hiba has a narrow meaning.

According to Ameer Ali, "A hiba is a voluntary gift without consideration of property or the substance of thing by one person to another so as to constitute the done the proprietor of the subject-matter of the gift." Muslim law allows a Muslim to give away his entire property by a gift inter-vivos, even with the specific object of disinheriting his heirs. [*Abdul vs. Ahmed,* (1881) 8 IA 25]

According to Mulla, "Gift is a transfer of property, made immediately, and without any exchange, by one person to another, and accepted by or on behalf of the latter".

According to Fyzee, "Hiba (Gift) is the immediate and unqualified transfer of the corpus of the property without any return".

Capacity to make a Hiba

Mental capacity – Every Muslim, male or female, married or unmarried, who has attained the age of majority and who is of sound mind has the mental capacity to make a gift. The rule of Muslim law of majority, *i.e.* attainment of puberty, does not apply to gifts. A person of unsound mind can make a valid gift during lucid intervals. The Muslim law-givers recognize the doctrine of ikrash or compulsion, and a gift-deed executed under compulsion is not valid. In such a case the gift is voidable, and it can be avoided by the donor whose consent was so obtained.

In the case of *Hussaina Bai vs. Zohara Bai,* [AIR 1960 MP 60] the validity of a gift made by parda-nasheen ladies was declared by the court. In this case, a parda-nasheen Muslim lady was brought from Nagpur to Burhanpur on an excuse that her brother-in-law was seriously ill. After reaching the place, she had a fit of hysteria, and soon after it, she was made to sign a gift deed without informing her the content of the deed and no opportunity was given to her to take an independent decision. The court held that-

"When a gift is made by a parda-nasheen lady, it is important to establish that the consent of the lady was free and she made the gift on her independent advice. The burden to prove that the gift was made free from compulsion lies on the donee. In this case, the deed was executed from the lady under

compulsion, it was not her voluntary act, and hence, the deed was held invalid."

Financial capacity – The *Malikis* hold the view that a person under insolvent circumstances or extremely involved circumstances have no capacity to make a gift. On the other hand, the Hanafis hold the view that insolvency does not create an incapacity to make a gift, but the kazi has the power to render such gift nugatory if it is made with a view to defrauding the creditors. The Indians court follow the Hanafi view. In every gift, there must be a bona fide intention on the part of the donor to transfer property to the donee. And, if a gift is made with an intention to defraud the creditors, the gift I invalid. *[Abdul vs. Mir Md,* (1886) 11 IA 10].

Essentials of a valid Gift (Hiba) : To make a gift valid, the following three essentials must co-exist :

(1) Declaration : When a gift is made with a clear and bonafide intention it is a valid gift. It is not necessary that this declaration must be made in writing. It may be made by words or conduct.

(2) Acceptance : It is also necessary that it must have been accepted by the donee or on behalf of him. The acceptance may be either express or implied (i.e., by conduct).

(3) Delivery of Possession : Delivery of Possession is an essential characteristics of a gift. The possession may be either actual or constructive. The actual possession may be given both of movable and immovable property. Money, Jewels, cloths and all tangible movable property must be actually transferred to the donee, mere entry in the books is not sufficient. In the case of an immovable property which is exclusive in the possession of the donor, it is necessary that the donor must physically depart from premises and hand it over to the donee.

The delivery of possession does not mean that the donor must have physical possession of the property and must hand over that physical possession to the donee. It is enough if he has got legal possession as the matter is susceptible of, as it was cited in the case of *Karim Bi vs. Mariam Bi,* AIR 1960 Mad. 447.

Exceptions to the General Rule : There are certain cases in which delivery of possession of the property is not necessary at all. These exceptions are as follows :

(1) Donor and Donee Reside in the same House: Where the donor and the donee reside in the same house, the donor can complete the gift without physical transfer of possession.

Recently, the Madras High Court in the case of *Ibrahim Bivi vs. Pakkir Mohideen,* (AIR 1970 Mad. 19) held that where the property gifted is a house and the settlor and the settle reside in that house, it is not necessary for the settlor formally to depart from the house in order to indicate that the settle has been given possession of the property gifted.

(2) Husband to Wife : Where a married couple lived in a house which belongs to the husband, the husband may make a gift of the house to the wife, without physical delivery of possession. The same rule is applicable in the case of a wife making a gift to the husband.

In *Amina Bibi vs. Khatija Bibi,* (SSC) (1864) 1 Bom.HCR 157, a husband had made a gift of his house to his wife. He has given the keys of the house to the wife, left the house for a few days, but had returned afterwards and lived with her till his death. It was held that the gift was valid.

(3) Guardian to Ward : Where a father or mother makes a gift of immovable property to their minor child, no physical transfer of possession is necessary. The same is rule between Guardian and Ward. But, if a gift is made to a minor by a person other than the father or guardian, delivery of possession to the father or guardian is necessary.

(4) Gift to Donee in Possession : Where the subject of the gift is already in the possession of the donee, the gift is complete by declaration and acceptant without formal delivery of possession.

Question No. 26

Who can make gifts and in whose favour a gift may be made - Explain ?

Answer :

Who can make Gift (Donor) : Every Muslim male or female who is a major and sane may make a gift, provided he or she is not subject to any force or fraud.

If the donor is suffering from the death-illness or Marz-ul-maut and in order to constitute the death-illness, it is essential that :—

(a) the illness must cause the death of the ill-person;

(b) the illness must cause apprehension of death in the mind of the deceased; and

(c) there must be some external symptoms of a serious illness.

A gift made during Marz-ul-Maut (death-illness) cannot take effect beyond one-third estate of the donor, after paying funeral expenses and debts, unless the heirs give consent, after the donor's death. Nor such a gift can take effect, if made in favour of an heir, unless the other heirs give their consent, after the donor's death.

A gift in death-illness takes place only when the donor dies. Such a gift is subejct to all conditions necessary for the validity of a simple gift, including delivery of possession by the donor to the donee.

In Whose Favour (Donee) : A gift may be made in favour of the following persons :—

(1) Any Living person who is capable of Holding Property : Strictly speaking, a gift to an unborn person is invalid. Take the example of A, who makes a gift to B, and after B's death, to his male heirs. B has got no male heirs at the time of the gift. The gift is invalid.

(2) Child in the Womb : A gift to an unborn person may be made provided the child is born within Six (6) months from the date of the gift, because in that case, it is presumed that the child was actually existing as a distinct entity in the womb.

(3) Unborn person : A gift of limited interest in the usufruct to property may be made to an unborn person provided that such person is in existence when the interest opens out for him.

(4) Juristic Persons : Gifts may be made validly to such juristic persons as Mosques, Dargahs, and charitable institutions, like schools, etc.

(5) Non-Muslims : A gift may be made to a non-Muslim. The gift property Will be subject to the personal law of the donee, once he gets possession of it.

(6) Two or More Persons : Where a gift is made to two or more persons (donees) without dividing the property, its validity is governed by the provisions of the Doctrine of Musha (undivided) share.

Question No. 27

Write a key note on the Revocation of the Gift ?

Answer :

According to Justice Ameer Ali, "The gift once completed can be revoked only by the intervention of the court of law or by consent of the donee".

Tyabji says, "All voluntary transactions including gifts are revocable".

There is a controversy of opinions in the different schools of Muslim Law regarding the revocation of the gift.

A revocation of gift can be studied under the following two headings :—

(a) Before Delivery of Possession.

(b) After Delivery of Possession

(a) Before Delivery of Possession : In fact, delivery of possession is the essential characteristic of a valid gift. So far the delivery of possession is not completed, the gift is not completed. The donor, may revoke the gift, before the delivery of possession of the property to the donee himself in present of the property and to confer it upon the donee.

In India, the Hiba-Bil-Iwaz is considered equally with that of a sale. Hence, it is required to be registered before the sub-

Registrar for the value exceeding Rs. 100/- as per Indian Registration Act and Indian Stamp Act.

Marz-Ul-Maut (Death Bed Gifts) : In literally sense, a gift made by a muslim during his death-bed, *i.e.,* at his last stage of life is called "Marz-ul-Maut" *i.e.* (Death-bed-Gift).

According to Baillie, "A gift is called Death-Bed Gift when the donor is suffering with death-illness.

Essentialities : (Important Points on Death Bed Gifts)

(1) The Donor's to dispose of his property by a gift during Marz-ul-Maut is limited to 1/3rd.

(2) The Limitation to a Will (Vasiyat) are also applicable to the gifts made during Marz-ul-Maut *i.e.,* (a) The donor cannot bequeath more than 1/3rd of his property, and (b) He cannot bequeath to his own heirs.

(3) In fact, a Death-Bed Gift is essentially a gift. It has all essentials of the gift *i.e.*;

(a) Declaration of the Donor;

(b) Acceptance of the Gift by or on behalf of the donee;

(c) Delivery of possession of the subject-matter of gift by the donor to the donee.

(b) After Delivery of Possession : Mere declaration of revocation by the donor, or institution of a suit, or any other action, is not sufficient to revoke a gift. Until a decree of the court is passed revoking the gift, the donee is entitled to use the property in any manner, he can also alienate it. [*Mahboob vs. Abdul,* 1964 Raj 250].

The revocation of a gift is a personal right of the donor, and, therefore, a gift cannot be revoked by his heirs after his death. A gift can also not be revoked after the death of the donee.

Under Hanafi Law, a gift once validly made is not revocable inthe following circumstances :—

(1) Where the donee is related to the donor within the prohibited degrees;

(2) Where the gift is made by the husband to his wife or vice versa during the subsistence of the marital relationship between them;

(3) Where the donee is dead and the subject-matter of the gift has devolved on his or heirs;

(4) Where the donor is dead;

(5) Where the thing given is lost or destroyed;

(6) Where the subject-matter of the gift has altered in substance in the hands of the donee. For example; wheat converted into flour;

(7) Where the gift is for a consideration; .

(8) Where the gift is of the debt to the debtor discharging the debtor from liability;

(9) Where the gift is "sadakh".

According to Shia law, a gift in favour of parents or in favour of consanguine relations cannot be lawfully be revoked. The revocation of gift is complete by a mere declaration without the sanction of the court.

Question No. 28

What are the Different Kinds of Gifts under Muslim Law ?

Answer :

Gifts (Hiba), in Muslim law, are of the following four kinds:

1. Sadaquah
2. Hiba-biliwaz
3. Hiba-ba-shart-ul-iwaz
4. Areeat

1. Sadaquah : Where the object of the donor is to acquire merit in the eyes of the Lord and a recompense in the next world, the gift is called Sadaquah. It is a gift with a religious motive. Like hiba, it is not valid unless accompanied by delivery of possession. Unlike hiba, it cannot be revoked, the reason being that the object of such a gift is acquisition of religious merit and that has already been acquired.

Sadaquah is a transfer of property or rights in all respects like a hiba, except that —

1. In the case of hiba, the object is to manifest affection towards the donee, or win his regard or esteem. In the case of sadaquah, the object is to acquire merit in the sight of the Lord and a recompense in the next world.

2. Unlike hiba, a sadaquah, once completed by delivery of possession, cannot be revoked, whether made to a rich or poor man.

3. Unlike hiba, sadaquah need not be expressly accepted.

2. Hiba-Bil-Iwaz : Hiba-bil-iwaz is a gift for a consideration. It resembles a sale in that (a) transfer of title is complete without delivery of possession, and (b) all the incidents of sale attach to it, including —(i) the liability of being pre-empted, where the law of pre-emption is in force, and (ii) the right to return a thing for a defect.

To constitute a valid Hiba-bil-iwaz, the following two conditions must be present:

(a) Actual and bona fide payment of consideration (iwaz) on the part of the donee; and

(b) A bona fide intention on the part of the donor to divest himself in praesenti of the property, and to confer it upon the donee.

3. Hiba-ba-Shart-ul-Iwaz : Where a gift is made with a stipulation (shart) for a return it is called hiba-ba-shart-ul-iwaz. As in the case of hiba, in the case of hiba- ba-shart-ul-iwaz also, delivery of possession is necessary, and the gift is revocable until the iwaz is paid. On payment of iwaz (consideration) by the donee, the gift becomes irrevocable. The transaction, when completed by payment of iwaz is, however, not very common in India.

4. **Areeat :** An areeat is the grant of a licence, revocable at the grantor's option, to take and enjoy the usufruct of a thing.

The four essentials of an areeat are that (i) can be revoked; (ii) it must be a transfer of ownership in the property; (iii) it must be for a definite period, and (iv) it does not devolve upon the heirs of the donee on his death.

Question No. 29

Explain the Doctrine of Musha, its rules and exceptions ?

Answer :

'Musha' has been defined as an undivided share in an immovable and movable property. Musha means 'Confusion'. An undivided share is called Musha because of the confusion that is likely to arise in the enjoyment of the property if a gift were made of an undivided share in the property by one co-sharer to stranger.

Rules Regarding Musha

(1) Property indivisible : The gift of an undivided share in property which does not admit of partition is valid. An undefine share in a small house or a small bath are mentioned as cases of Musha, a gift of whch would be valid.

(2) Property divisible : The gift of an undivided share in any property capable of division is, with certain exception, incomplete and irregular, although it can be rendered valid by subsequent separation and delivery of possession. This is the rule of Hanafi Law, but in Shafei Law, the gift of Musha is valid provided the donor withdrew his donation over the property and permits the donee to exercise control.

The Doctrine of Musha is subject to the following exceptions :

(1) Gift to co-heir : This doctrine is not applicable where one co-heir makes a gift to another, A Muslim woman died leaving a mother, a son and a daughter. The mother made a gift of her unrealised 1/6th share jointly to the deceased's son and daughter. The gift is valid.

(2) Co-shares in undivided land or zamindaries : Justice Amir Ali says that the doctrine of Musha was applicable only to small plots of land and not to specific shares in large landed properties like zamindaries. But the modern rule is that in this case the rule as to Musha does not apply.

(3) Gift to two or more persons : If the shares of the donees are clearly and distinctly specified a gift to two or more persons jointly is valid, notwithstanding that the donor has not divided the property by metes and bounds, and handed over the specific shares to each donee.

(4) Where the property is freehold property in large commercial towns.

(5) The shares in a landed company are not subject to the rule regarding Musha.

(6) If it is made to the poor, or it is the nature of Sadaqa the gift of Musha is valid.

(7) Where the right to receive separately a definite share of the rents of some undivided property is transferred. Where property is transferred by way of gift and the donor does not reserve dominion over the corpus of the property nor any share of dominion over the corpus but stipulates simply for and obtains a right to the recurring income during his life, the gift and stipulation both are valid.

Shia Law : Shia law does not recognise the doctrine of Mushaa. Under the Shia law, a gift of a share of divisible joint property is valid even if made without partition.

Question No. 30

Distinguish between Hiba and Ariya ?

Answer :

This differences between Hiba (Gift) and Ariya (usufruct) are given below

S.	Hiba (Gift)	Ariya (Usufruct)
1.	The donor must be a person who has attained majority.	Majority not essential
2.	Ownership of the property shall be transferred.	It the transfer of the use of Ariya (usufruct) only and not the ownership.
3.	It must not be conditional or limited in time.	It may be subject to conditions limiting the duration of use.
4.	It must be immediate and not contingent.	It may be in future.
5.	Gift of Musha cannot be made except in few cases.	Doctrine of Musha does not apply
6.	Acceptance is necessary for its completion.	Acceptance is not a condition.

Question No. 31

Write an essay on Wassiyat – Wills under Muslim Law?

Answer :

A Wassiyat or will under Muslim law is a divine institution, since its exercise is regulated by Koran. Will is the translation of Latin word "voluntas", which was a term used in the text of the Roman law to express the intention of a testator. Under Muslim law, every Muslim has the testamentary power of disposing of his property. But his testamentary power is limited to the disposal of only one-third of his property.

A Wassiyat offers to the testator the means of correcting to a certain extent the law of succession, and of enabling some of those relatives who are excluded from inheritance to obtain a share in his goods, and/or recognizing the services rendered to him by a stranger, or the devotion to him in his last moments." This seems to be the reason why the word "Wassaya" or "Wassiyat" has two meanings; it means a will and it also signifies a moral exhortation. The word Wassiyat also means a specific legacy or the capacity of the executor.

Definitions of Will :—(1) According to Tayabji, Will means "The declaration of the intentions of a Muslim with respect to his property, which he desires to be carried into effect after his death".

(2) According to Hedaya, "Wassiyat (Will) means an endowment with the property of anything after death—as if one person should say to another, give this article of mine, after my death, to a particular person".

(3) In General, the Will means, "it is an instrument by which a person makes a disposition of his property to take effect after his decease and which is in its own nature and also revocable during his life".

Who can make Wills : A Muslim who is a of sound mind and is major can make a will. Although according to Muslim Law, majority is dependent upon the age of puberty which is supposed to reached at fifteen (15) years of age, yet the Indian Majority Act recognizes only the age of eighteen (18) years as a requisite for the purposes of will.

A minor may make a Will, but its validity would be postponed to the event when, after attaining majority, he ratifies it, but such a will is very weak.

A will made by a person after he has taken poison or has done any other act towards the commission of suicide, is not valid. The Shia law, however, says that if the person made the Will and then committed suicide, the bequest would be valid.

For whom the bequest can be made : (1) Any person : Any person who is capable of holding property, whether male or female, Muslim or non-muslim, may validty avail the benefit of a bequest.

(2) Unborn person : Unborn person cannot be a legatee. however, if the legatee is in the womb and the birth takes place within six months from the date of making the Will, he can be a lawful legatee. Shia Law recognizes a legatee born within ten (10) months from the date of Will.

(3) Heirs : Heirs cannot be the legatees, that is, no bequest to heirs, who are entitled to inherit. This rule is relaxed only in cases, where other heirs give their consent (after testator's death in Hanafi Law, and before or after testator's death, in Shia Law). By giving consent, an heir can bind only his own share but not of others.

It is very essential that the heir must be in existence at the time of testator's death consent may be inferred from the conduct of heirs.

Formalities of a Wassiyat or Will : Muslim law requires no specific formalities for the execution of a will. A will may be oral or in writing. When the will is in writing, no specific form is laid down. It may not even be signed by the testator or attested by the witnesses. [*Ramjilal vs. Ahmed,* 1952 MB 56] However, it is necessary that the intention of the testator should be clear and unequivocal. In *Mazhar vs. Bodha,* 21 All 91 a letter was written by a Muslim shortly before his death, containing directions for the disposition of his property, was accepted to constitute a valid will.

When a will is oral, no form of declaration is necessary. Obviously, the burden of establishing an oral will is very heavy, and an oral will must be proved with utmost precision and with every circumstance of time and place. [*Venkat vs. Namdeo,* (1931) 58 IA 362].

Modes of Revocation of Will :

A bequest may be revoked by the testator either expressly or impliedly or by a subsequent Will.

(1) Express Revocation : It is one where the testator revokes the bequest in express terms either orally or in writing. But a mere denial by the testator that he did not make a will does not act as revocation of an otherwise valid will.

(2) Implied Revocation : It is one where the testator does an act from which revocation may be inferred.

(3) Subsequent Will : A bequest to a person is revoked by a bequest in a subsequent will of the same property to another person.

Question No. 32

Write the differences between Sunni (Hanafi) and Shia Law in regard to Will ?

Answer :

Sunni (Hanafi) Law	Shia Law
1. Hanafi Law disqualifies an heir from being a legatee when the other heirs do not consent to the legacy in favour of the heir.	Shia Law allows even a heir to be legatee upto the legal 1/3rd, which can be disposed of by Will. It is only for a disposition beyond this 1/3rd limit that Shia law requires the consent of the other heirs.
2. Under the Sunni Law, the other heirs may gie their consent for the *wasiyyat* beyond 1/3rd of the estate before the testator's death and it will be invalid if it is given after the testator's death.	Under the Shia Law, the cosnent of the other heirs, may be given either before or after the death of the tstator if the limit exdceeds the legal one-third of the subject. The consent of the other heirs even in testator's lifetime would validate it.
3. Under the Hanafi Law if the legatee predeceases the testator, the legacy fails.	Under the Shia Law, the heir of the legatee can claim legacy if the legatee predeceases the testatgor.

Sunni (Hanafi) Law	Shia Law
4. When more than 1/3rd is disposed of and the heirs do not consent, under the hanafi law there is a proportionate abatement of all the legacies affected thereby.	When more than 1/3rd is disposed of and the heirs under the Shia law the legatees take in the order in which the legacies are granted upto the disposable 1/3rd and the later legacies fail altogether.
5. Under the Sunni law bequest in excess of the legal third in favour of a non-heir cannot take effect unless the heirs consent thereto after the testator's death.	Under Shia law the consent is necessary to validate a bequest in exces:of the legal third in favour of a non-heir may be given either before or after the testator's death.
6. According to Sunni School a legacy in favour of an heir, whatever the amount, is invalid unless the other heirs consent therein.	In the Shia School of law legacies in favour of an heir to the extent of one-third aare allowed with-out the cosnent of the other heirs.
7. If a person of whom legacy is made by the testator dies before the testatgor himself, it will lapse and become part of the estate of the testator under Sunni law.	If a person of whom legacy is made by the testator dies before the testator himself, it willlapse and become part of the estate of the testator under Sunni law.

Sunni (Hanafi) Law	Shia Law
8. Life estates are not recognised in Sunni law.	Life estates not recogni-sed in Shia law.
9. A Will of a person committing suicide is valid in Sunni law.	Under Shia law if a person wounds himself mortally, or takes poison for committing suicide or otherwise takes any step towards committing suicide and then makes a Will, such a Will is invalid.
10. Under Sunni law, a Will to a person who cause the death of the testator is void even when it is caused unintentionally.	Under the Shia law, a bequest to a person who cause the death of the testator is void and causes forfeiture of legacy only when the death is caused unintentionally.
11. Under Sunni law, if the bequest exceeds the legal one-third and the heirs refuse their cosnent the bequest abates rateably.	Under the Shia law, there is no rateable abatement. Bequests prior in date take priority over those that are later in date.
12. Under Sunni law, a be-quest to a child in womb is valid if born within 6 months.	Under the Shia law, bequest is valid even if born in the longest period of question, *i.e.*, 10 months.
13. Under Sunni law, acceptance of the legacy before the testator's death is of no effect.	Under Shia law, accep-tance of the legacy during the testator's lifetime is a lawful.

Question No. 33

Define Executor. State the powers and conditions of the Executor ?

Answer :

Executor

Meaning of Executor : The testator is fully empowered to appoint any one irrespective of sex and religion as the executor to execute his last wishes. A Muslim may appoint a Christian, a Hindu and any nonMuslim as his executor. According to Fatawa-e-Khazi Khan, the executor is bound to carry out the wishes of the testator which are valid in law with utmost fidelity, to safeguard the interests of testator and to administer his estate. The executor may be appointed for a specific purpose or for general purpose.

According to Fatawa-e-Alamgiri, when an infant or an insane person, is appointed, as an executor whether permanently or with lucide intervals, it is not valid.

A minor can be associated with an adult executor in the office but he has no power to interfere in the administration of the State until he has attained puberty. The adult executor can act alone until the minor attains puberty.

A slave may be appointed as executor.

A testator may appoint any person subject to certain qualifications as the executor of his Will and such appointment will be effective from the date of acceptance by the executgor. Such acceptance may be express or implied and it may take place either during the lifetime of testator or after his death. An executor is empowered to refuse to accept the ofice, and he may also renounce the same at any time.

If onece the executorship is accepted and the property of a legatee is dealt with in accordance with the terms of Will the executor cannot renounce his office unless sanction is accorded by a Judge.

An executor may be appointed under Shia law in any manner which indicate the intention of the testator to make him as executor. More than one person can be appointed as executor.

Under the Shia law when joint executors are appointed one of them can act singly unelss his acts are positively incumbent or necessary. They may lawfully divide the property of the testator between them and each one can take upon himself the management of such divided proeprty.

Under the Hanafi rules governing Wills, when more than one person are appointed as joint executors one cannot act individually in disposing of the property of testator.

Powers and functions of executors : According to Hidaya, when the heirs of the testators are minors the powers of the executor are absolute, but within certain limits. The executor has the power of selling the property and invest the sale proceeds if there is necessity to do so and such a step should be taken only after discharging the debts of the testator, if any, and after making maintenance to the minor children of the testator. The sale must be for an adequate consideration.

According to Durrul Mukhtar, the executor has no power to sell the proeprty of the testator, to himself or to any of his relatives.

According to Durrul Mukhtar and Fatawa-e-Alamgiri it is lawful for the executor to sell otgher than immovable property against an absent adult heir to pay the debts of the testator and even the sale of immovable property is valid if it is apprehended that it will be lost. If the deceased dies heavily indebted, then by cosnensus a sale of immovable proeprty is valid.

Acciording to Fatawa-e-Alamgiri, if the executors sell the estate for the payment of the debts of the deceased which do not cover the entire estate, it is lawful.

According to Shia law an executor is not responsible for anyloss of destruction of the proeprty of the testator unless occasioned by his departure from the conditions of his office.

Relating to executor, the Law of Beqwuests compiled by All India Muslim Personal Law Board in its Chapter 2 provides that :

"An executor is a personh nominated by the legator for taking care of his minor or insane children, distributionof the estate, executoion of bequestgs, and protectionof assets, etc. after his death. [Section 24]

If a person has not appointed an executor, the *qazi* will have the authority to appoint someone as the executor for fulfilling the purposes mentioned in Section 24 above. The person nominated byteh legator is called teh 'real executor' or 'legator's executor', and the one appointed byteh *qazi* the 'judicial executor'. [Section 25].

Conditions for executor : A person to be appointed as the executor must have the following qualities: (i) being a Muslim; (ii) sanity; (iii) majority; and (iv) capability. [Section 26]

If a person is nominated as an executor in violation of the aforestated conditions, it will be obligatory for the *qazi* to appoint another person fulfilling the said conditions. [Section 27].

The executor may or may not be a relative. [Section 28]

If after the legator has made the bequestg the executor has not rejected the executorship and has agreed toit in the prsence or knowledge of the legator, or inhis absence or ignorance, or after his death in thepresence of some prsons, in all these cases of acceptance the executor cannot now be relieved of his responsibility, except if he rejects it in the legator's knowledge, or if the legatgor has died, in the presence and with the cosnent of the *qazi*. [Section 29].

If an executor who did not refuse his assignment and had kept quiet during the legator's life time, rejects it after his death, but before the rejection is approved bythe *qazi* expresses his acceptance, the acceptance will be valid and he will be regarded as tghe executor. [Section 30].

If an executor had kept quiet during the legator's life time but begins discharging his responsibilities after his death, this is acceptance by conduct on his part. [Section 31].

Rearing, education and training of the legator's children will be the legatee's foremost obligation. [Section 32].

The legator can at anytime remove the executor appointed by him. [Section 33].

If the executor is unable to perform in full all his assigned jobs, the *qazi* will add more persons for the performance of those jobs as may be necessary. [Section 34].

If the executor is wholly unable to perform the assigned jobs, the qazi shall remove him and appoint another person in his place as the executor. [Section 35].

If one of the two executors appointed bythe deceased dies and the deceased executor has not on his part named the suriving executor or a third person as the executor, in such a situation the qazi will nominate another executor along with the surviving executor. [Section 36].

If the deceased had appointed two executors, or if there is one executor appointed by the deceased and anoher by the qazi (in those cases where it is lawful for the qazi to appoint an executor), neither of them can have any dealing without the consent of the other, except in some special situation. [Section 38].

If the two executors are in agreement that the legator's estate will remain in the custody of either of them or a third person, it will be so; and in the case of difference of opinion each executor will take custody of half of the heritable estate, and the impartible property will remian in the custodyof both turn by turn for specific periods. [Section 39].

If an executor says to a person "I appoint you my executor", this other executor will be the custodian of the goods, property and affairs of the first legator as well, and will be entitled to deal with the property and goods also of the person who has appointed him, *i.e.* the second legator. However, he will have the right to deal with the property and goods of either of them only if so specified by the appointing executor. [Section 40].

The executor cannot sell the movable or immovable proeprty of the legator except for extreme necessity; and in a case of extreme necessity sales will begin with imovable property.

Explanation : 'Extreme necessity' refers to the necessities relating to the legator's property and goods, or to his family members. [Section 41].

If the deceased has left no debt and no bequest and all his heirs are major and are present, the executor shall not in such a situation take any step in respect of any matter relating to the legator's property and goods without the express consent of the legator's heirs. However, if the heirs are avoiding discharge of debts payable by the legator, or payment of lawful legacis left by him, the executor will perform both these functions. [Section 42].

An executor appointed by the mother can sell, if necessary, only the movable property inherited by the minors out of her estate, provided that the father or the grandfather has not appointed an executor. [Section 43].

The executor appointed buy the mother can sell movable things inherited out of her estate if necessary for the payment of debts and for the execution of the bequest. [Section 44].

It is not lawful for the executor or his family to benefit in any way from the legator's property, neither by raising loans on it nor by using it for business. [Section 45].

The executor can lawfully appoint a representative to act on his behalf in respect of transactions. The representative so apponted by him will automaticaly vacate his position on the executor's death or on the children becoming major. [Section 46].

It will not be valid for the executor to acknowledge existence of a debt or legacy on the part of the legator. [Section 47].

If an heir of the deceased acknowledges a legacy left by the latter while the other heirs deny it, the acknowledgement by the acknowledging heir will be limited in its effect only to his share in the estate of the deceased and will not in any way affect the shares of the other heirs. [Section 48].

If an executor pays an alleged debt of the deceased for which the claimant had no witness or evidence, nor any decision of the quazi of affirmation by the heirs, he will be laible to compensate for it. [Section 49].

If the legator has not fixed up any honorarium for the executor, it will be lawful for the latter to take a suitable honourarium in the customary way from the property of the legatgor's minor children.

A decision by the qazi will be a cautious and safe way for the determination of the quantum of honorarium. [Sectin 50].

Question No. 34

Distinction between Will and Gift ?

Answer :

Both Will and gift are modes of transferring property from the person making the gift or will to the person in whose favour it is made. The main point of distinction between the two is that while 'gift' is a transfer of property made immediately 'Will' is a "transfer of property to take after the death of the testator".

Basis of Comparison	Gift	Will
Quantum	A man can give away his whole property during his lifetime.	Only one-third of the net estate can be bequeathed.
Beneficiary	A gift inter vivos can be made in favour of any person without any restriction (except during marz-ul-maut).	For bequeathing more than one-third of the property to any person, consent of heirs is mandatory.
Existence of Property	Property gifted must be in existence at the time of making the gift.	The property may or may not be in existence at the time of execution of the will but it must be existing at the time of the death of the legator.

Transfer of Property	Under gift, the immediate and absolute transfer of property takes place.	A transfer of property comes into effect only after the death of the legator.
Delivery of Possession	Immediate delivery of possession must take place as soon as the donor declares the gift and the donee accept the same.	Since property devolves on the legatee only after the death of the legator so no question of delivery of possession arises.
Revocation	Once a gift is made, a mere declaration to revoke it by the donor is not sufficient. A revocation can only take place either by the consent of the donee or by the intervention of the court.	A bequest may be revoked by the legator any time after executing it and before his death either impliedly or expressly or by a subsequent will.

———

UNIT -- IV

WAQF

Question No. 35

Define Waqf. Discuss the Essentials ?

A Waqf under Muslim law is essentially a religious and pious obligation, though provision is sometimes also made for charities and for the benefit of oneself, one's children and descendants (alal-aulad). The origin of Waqf is traced to an utterance of the Prophet. The utterance is often quoted and is considered the briefest definition of Waqf – "Tie up the substance and give away the fruit". However, in early days of Islam, the law of Waqfs suffered from great uncertainty. It was only in the second century after the flight that a body of rules based on ijma (consensus) were developed which might be considered to be the basis of the law of Waqfs.

In the centuries that followed not merely the land but all type property, movable and immovable were made the subject matter of Waqfs. In the course of time, the Muslims world found that the "dead hand" (as Waqfs were figuratively called and which in fact they had become) was trying to strangulate all progress and prosperity. Vast stretches of land and all other types of properties were dedicated to Waqfs all over the Muslims world. In India, there are about one lakh Waqfs valued at more than a hundred crores of rupees.

Instances of the mismanagement of the Waqfs are numerous; the incompetence and corruption of the mutawallis are appalling and abysmal; more often than not, the properties of the Waqfs are squandered away.

Under Muslim law, there are several religious institutions for which a Waqf can be created. Important among them are a mosque, graveyard, dargah, takia, khanqah, and imambara.

Definition of Waqf : The word Waqf literally means 'detention'. Abu Hanifa defined Waqf as "the tying up of the substance of a property in the ownership of the wakif and the devotion of the usufruct, amounting to an aryia, or commodate loan for some charitable purpose." This means that, according to him, the ownership in Waqf property continued to be vested in the owner, and its usufruct was spent for the charitable or pious purpose. Also, he believed that the tying up of the property was not of a permanent nature. His two disciples, however, took a different view.

According to Abu Yusuf and Imam Mohammed, Waqf is the "tying up of the substance of a thing under the rule of the property of Almighty God for any purpose by which its profit may be applied for the benefit of His creatures." However, Muhammed thought that the right of the wakif was not extinguished until he appointed a muttawali, while Abu Yusuf took the view that the right of the wakif was extinguished the moment he made the declaration.

Abu Yusuf's definition came to be established in view of the Waqf and of the Hanafi School. The definition of Waqf has three essential elements :

1. The ownership of the wakif is extinguished;
2. The property is vested in the ownership of God perpetually and irrevocably; and
3. The usufruct of the property is used for the benefit of the mankind.

The Shia law defines a Waqf in a different manner. According to Sharia-ul-Islam, a Waqf is a contract, the fruit or effect of which is to tie up the original of a thing and to leave its usufruct free.

The Waqf Act, 1913, Section 2, defines Waqf. Accordingly, it means the permanent dedication by a person professing the Mussalman faith of any property for any purpose recognized by the Mussalman law as religious, pious or charitable. Thus the purpose must be religious, pious, or charitable, the dedication of property must be permanent, and the usufruct must be utilized for the good of mankind. [*Kani Ammal vs. Tamil Nadu Waqf Board* [1983 AP 188].

Objects of Waqfs : Objects of a Waqf may be religious and charitable or private.

(1) Religious and Charitable Objects : Religious and charitable objects of Waqf are so intimately connected with each other that sometimes it may not be possible to make a distinction between them.

It is well settled that the object of Waqf should not be in conflict with the generally religious policy of Islam. Religious purposes, however, do not include such dedications as "solely to the worship of God", which is "an un-meaning phrase in Islam" says Ameer Ali, commenting on a Bombay High Court decision in the case of *Abdul Gani Kasim vs. Hussain Miya,* (10 Bom.HCR 10).

Charitable objects include giving to one's own family and descendants, and such things in which rich and poor may be equally interested. For example : Mosque, Imambara; Dargah; Kangah, College and School; Hospital; Reservoir, Roads and Bridges, etc.

(2) Private Waqfs

Waqfs in favour of one's own family may be termed as private Waqfs. They may be :

(a) exclusively for the family; or

(b) substantially for the family with some provision for charity; or

(c) substantially for charity with some provision for the family.

Exclusively for Family : Delivering the judgment in *Bikani Mian vs. Shukh Lal Poddar,* (1893) 20 Cal. 116, Mr. Justice Ameer Ali observed that a Waqf exclusively for the benefit of Waqf's (person creating Waqf) family without any provision for charity, was valid.

Essentials/Characteristics of a Waqf

. **Property vests in god** – Once the dedication of the property is made to the Waqf, the ownership of the Waqf is transferred to god. [*Md. Ismalia vs. Thakur Sabif Ali,* 1962 SC 1722] Under the Shia law also the property of Waqf vests in god. Thus it seems to be that in respect of Waqf property in god there is no distinction between a Shia Waqf and Sunni Waqf or a public Waqf or private Waqf.

. **Waqf must be Permanent** – A Muslim Waqf must be created for an unlimited period. In short, perpetuity is an essential feature of a Waqf. Even in the case of a family Waqf, the ultimate benefit must be expressly or impliedly reserved for the poor or for any other purpose of a permanent character. [*Rahlman vs. Bagridan,* 1936 Oudh 213]

. **Waqf must be Irrevocable –** The irrevocability is another characteristic feature of a Waqf. Once constituted validly, a Waqf cannot be revoked. If in a Waqfnama a conditions is stipulated that the wakif reserves to him the right of revoking the Waqf or the Waqf will stand revoked on the happening of any event, then such a Waqf is void. [*Asoobai vs. Noorbai,* (1906) 8 Bom LR 18].

. **Waqf properties are Inalienable –** Once a property is dedicated to the god, they can't be alienated. However this rule is not absolute and in some circumstances, it is permissible that a mutawalli may alienate the Waqf properties, a mutawalli may sell or grant a lease of the Waqf properties with the prior permission of the court. When a Waqfnama allows selling Waqf properties in some circumstances, then the mutawalli has the power to alienate Waqf properties in those circumstances.

Broadly, a Waqfs are of two kinds :

(1) Public and

(2) Private.

But the most accepted is its threefold classification—(a) Private (b) Quasi-Public and (c) Private.

(a) Public Waqfs : Those which are dedicated to the public at large having no restriction of any kind regarding its use; for example, Bridges, well, Roads, etc.

(b) Quasi-Public Waqfs : Those which are partly public and partly to provide for the benefit of a particular individual or class of individuals which may be the settlor's family.

Those which are partly public and partly to provide for the benefit of a particular individual or class of individuals which may be the settlor's family.

(c) Private Waqfs : Those which are for the benefit of private individuals, including the settlor's family or relation. Such Waqf is termed as 'Waqf-Al-Aulad.

Muslim Law gives equal recognition to public and private Waqfs.

Legal Incidents Of Waqf

There are three legal incidents of Waqf :

(a) Irrevocability (b) Perpetuity (c) Inalienability

(a) Irrevocability : According to Abu Hanifa, a Waqf can be revoked by its founder unless the declaration has been confirmed by a court decree. However, Abu Yusuf took a contrary view and held that a declaration of Waqf is, in its nature, irrevocable. That is, a Waqf cannot be revoked after the declaration has been made, nor can the power to revoke be validly reserved. It is the opinion of Abu Yousuf which prevails in India.

(b) Perpetuity : Waqf must be perpetual. If it is for a limited period or for a temporary purpose, it is void.

(c) Inalienability : As the Waqf belongs to God, no human being can alienate it for his own purposes. Consequently, Waqf property cannot be the subject of sale, mortgage, gift, inheritance or any alienation whatsoever. This general rule has two exceptions, Waqf property may be exchanged for an equivalent property, or sold, subject to compulsory re-investment of the price is another property. The power of exchange and sale in subject to the permission of the court.

Question No. 36

Discuss about the Creation and Revocation of Waqf?

Answer :

A Waqf under Muslim law is essentially a religious and pious obligation, though provision is sometimes also made for charities and for the benefit of oneself, one's children and descendants (alal-aulad). The origin of Waqf is traced to an utterance of the Prophet. The utterance is often quoted and is considered the briefest definition of Waqf – "Tie up the substance and give away the fruit". However, in early days of Islam, the law of Waqfs suffered from great uncertainty. It was only in the second century after the flight that a body of rules based on ijma (consensus) were developed which might be considered to be the basis of the law of Waqfs.

Any Muslim who has attained the age of majority i.e. 18 years, and who is of sound mind, may make a Waqf. A Waqf cannot be made by a guardian on behalf of the minor, such a Waqf is void. [*Commissioner of Waqf vs. Md. Mohsin,* (1953) 58 Cal WN 252].

The Mussalman Waqf Validating Act, 1913, and the Waqf Act, 1954, contemplate that a Waqf can be made only by a Muslim. Similarly, the Waqf Act, 1954, defines a Waqf as meaning a permanent dedication by a person professing Islam. But the Nagpur High Court has expressed the view that a non-muslim can also make a Waqf – the law only requires that "the object should be lawful and in consonance with Islam". [*Moti Shah vs. Abdul Gaffar,* 1953 Nag 38].

Muslim law does not recognize any form of creating a Waqf. A Waqf may be made in writing or may be oral. There must be appropriate words to show an intention to dedicate the property. The use of the word Waqf is neither necessary nor conclusive. To constitute a Waqf it is not necessary that the word 'Waqf' should be used. A grant to the Kazi is compulsory for the purposes of his performing religious or pious duties to constitute a Waqf.

1. **By an act inter vivos** – It means during the lifetime. Thus a Waqf is created during the lifetime of the wakif and takes effect from that very time.

2. **By will** – It stands in contradiction with the Waqf. It takes effect after the death of the wakif and also called testamentary Waqf. A Waqf by will cannot operate upon more than one-third of net assets, without the consent of the heirs.

3. **During death illness (Marz-ul-maut)** – The Waqf made during the deadly illness will operate only to the extent of one-third of the property without the consent of the heirs of the wakif.

4. **By immemorial user** – Waqf may be established by evidence of immemorial user. For e.g. when a land has been from time immemorial use for the purpose of a burial ground, it is a Waqf by the immemorial user.

Statutory control over Waqfs – The Waqf Act, 1995

It is no longer a secret that the most of the religious institutions are badly managed and bad management of Waqf with regards to their funds and abuse of the setup have reached menacing proportions.

The Government of India being aware of this state of affairs passed the Waqf Act, 1923. During the British rule, several provinces passed statutes to control the management of religious institutions. Some of these applied to Waqf also. But things did not improve. The Waqf Act, 1923 was replaced by Waqfs Act, 1954, which was amended in 1964. But things still did not improve much. Parliament then passed the Waqf Act, 1995 for the better administration of Waqfs and connected matters thereof.

The Act provides for the survey of all Waqfs and registration of Waqfs. A Central Waqf Council is stipulated to be established for overseeing, advising and looking after the working of Waqf Boards. The Act is also stipulated to establish Waqf Boards in each state, if necessary, separate Waqf Board of Shia and Sunni Waqfs. The Waqf Board is the main instrumentality for the management of Waqfs.

Registration of Waqfs (Section 36, The Waqf Act, 1995)

The Act makes registration of every Waqf compulsory. Mutawallis of Waqfs are required to move an application for registration of Waqfs. Such an application can also be made by a Waqf or his descendants or a beneficiary of a Waqf. The application should state the following particulars:

1. a description of the Waqf properties sufficient for the identification thereof;

2. the gross annual income from such properties;

3. the amount of land revenue, cesses, rates and taxes annually payable in respect of the Waqf properties;

4. an estimate of the expenses annually incurred in the realisation of the income of the Waqf properties;

5. the amount set apart under the Waqf for—

(a) the salary of the mutawalli and allowances to the individuals;

(b) purely religious purposes;

(c) charitable purposes; and

(d) any other purposes;

(e) any other particulars provided by the Board by regulations.

Revocation of Waqf : A Waqf when complete is irrevocable. The Waqf cannot reserve the power to revoke the Waqf or to withdraw any property from the Waqf.

A testamentary Waqf *i.e.*, a Waqf made by Will, may be revoked by the Waqf at any time before his death. A Waqf created during Marz-ul-maut (Death-illness) and testamentary Waqf stand on the same footing.

Question No. 37

What are the differences between Shia and Sunni Law regarding Waqf ?

Answer :

The following are the points of difference between Shia Law and Sunni Law regarding Waqf :

Shia Law	Sunni Law
1. Under Shia Law property vests in beneficiaries.	1. While under Sunni Law the property vests in God.
2. Under Shia Law Waqf is irrevocable after possession given to beneficiaries.	2. Under Sunni Law Waqf is irrevocable, unless (a) there is decree of court, or (b) it is testamentary.
3. Under Shia Law Waqf must not purport to be limited to a fixed period of time.	3. Under Sunni Law Waqf must expressly purport to be in perpetuity.
4. Under Shia Law if the object of Waqf fails, the property reverts to the Waqif of his heirs.	4. Under Sunni Law if the object of waqf fails, or is such that it may fail, waqf is void.
5. Under Shia Law the provision for payment of personal debts not charged on the property is not permitted.	5. Under Sunni Law waqf may provide for payment of his personal debts.

6. Under Shia Law a waqif may appoint a Mutawalli before he transfers possession but after that in the absence of any provision in the deed, the beneficiaries are entitled to administer the Waqf.	6. While under Sunni Law, in the absence of provision in the deed of waqf, the Waqif is entitled to be Mutawalli and may appoint a person in case of a vacancy.

Question No. 38

Write a short note on Mutawalli

Answer :

Mutawalli means the Manager or superintendent of the Waqf. The moment a Waqf is created, all rights of property pass out of the Waqf and vest in the Almighty. The Waqf property is vested in God and the Mutawalli is considered as a manager of Waqf property. he has no estate or interest int eh Waqf property. A Mutawalli may be any person of sound mind and who has attained majority may be appointed a Mutawalli.

Under the Mohammedan law, the moment a wakf is created, all rights of property pass out of the wakif and is vested in God. The property is then taken care of by a Mutawalli. A Mutawalli is more like a manager than a trustee and so far as the wakf property is concerned, he has to see that the beneficiaries get the advantage of the usufruct. All the beneficiaries are entitled to benefit equally subject to any special power conferred on the Mutawalli. The statement in Mulla's 'Mohammedan Law' that a "Mutawalli is not a mere superintendent or manager but is practically speaking the owner" is not correct. [*Bibi Saddiqa Fatima vs. Saiyed Mohd. Mahmood Hasan,* AIR 1978 SC 1362].

A mutawalli is not entitled to any remuneration as of right. The wakif may provide for remuneration for the mutawalli.

Who is appointed as a Mutawalli : Any person of sound mind who has attained the age of majority can be appointed as a mutawalli. [*Syed Hasan vs. Mir Hasan,* (1917) 40 Mad. 543] A minor may be a mutawalli where the office of mutawalli is hereditary and the person entitled to succeed is a minor, or where the line of succession is laid down in the wakf-nama and the office falls on a minor. [*Piran vs. Abdool Karim,* (1891) 19 Cal 203].

Both male and female of any religion can be appointed as a mutawalli. The mutawalli must be capable of performing the particular duties under the wakf. If religious duty or spiritual functions are a part of the duties of a mutawalli, a female and non-muslim cannot be appointed as a mutawalli. [*Shahar Bano vs. Aga Mahommad,* (1907) 34 I.A. 46] Thus a woman or a non-muslim cannot be Sajjadanashin (spiritual head), Khatib (one who reads sermons), Mujawar of a dargah, an Imam of a mosque (one who leads congression) or a mulla. A foreigner cannot be the trustee of any wakf property in India.

Modes of the Appointment of Mutawalli : Ordinarily, there are three modes of the appointment of Mutawalli which are as under :-

(1) A mutawalli may be appointed by the Waqf or by the wakif or by some person expressly authorised by the wakif to appoint and, in the absence of any person so authorised.

(2) He may be appointed by the executor of the Waqf, and in the absence of any person so authorised.

(3) Appointed by the court : The power of appointment is vested in the District Court. When the court appoints a mutawalli, it will take into consideration: (i) the direction, if any, given by the founder (the court has the discretion to disregard any direction of the wakif it feels that to do so will be to the manifest advantage of the wakf) (ii) Preference should be given to a member of the wakif's family over an utter stranger. (iii) In a contest between wakif's lineal descendant

and one who is not a lineal descendant, the court is free to exercise its discretion.

Can Following Persons Be Appointed as Mutawalli:

(1) A Minor : A minor cannot be appointed as Mutawalli. But where the office of the Mutawalli is hereditary and the person entitled to succeed to the office is a minor, the person entitled to succeed to the office on the death of the first or other Mutawalli Will act in his place during his minority.

(2) A woman and Non-Muslim: A woman or non-muslim can be appointed as a mutawalli. But where the mutawalli was to perform religious duties or spiritual functions which cannot be performed by a woman or a non-muslim.

Removal of a Mutawalli : A Mutawalli once appointed cannot be removed by the wakif, unless such power was reserved by hm in the deed or Waqf. The court is, however, entitled to remove a mutawalli for manifest malversation or on the ground of physical or mental incapacity or gross incompetence or dereliction of duty or proving his fitness for the office which he holds. However, the Mutawalli can only be removed by means of a suit properly instituted in the Civil Court.

Once a wakf comes into existence and a mutawalli is appointed, the founder has no power of removing him unless such a power has been specifically reserved in the wakf deed. [*Siddique Ahmed vs. Syed Ahmed, 1945 Cal 418*].

The court has a power to remove a mutawalli. A court may remove a mutawalli on the ground of misfeasance, breach of trust or for his unfitness, or for any valid reason. The court's power of removal is unfettered, and it can remove a mutawalli even if the settlor has specifically laid down that the mutawalli should not be removed. It is because the foremost duty of the court is to consider the interest of the wakf. Procedure for removing a mutawalli is by way of a suit in the District Court. [*Md. Ali vs. Ahmad Ali,* 1946 All 261 Cl 328].

Question No. 39

Explain the powers and duties of a Mutawalli ?

Answer :

Mutawalli means the Manager or superintendent of the Waqf. The moment a Waqf is created, all rights of property pass out of the Waqf and vest in the Almighty. The Waqf property is vested in God and the Mutawalli is considered as a manager of Waqf property. He has no estate or interest int eh Waqf property. A Mutawalli may be any person of sound mind and who has attained majority may be appointed a Mutawalli.

(a) Powers of Mutawalli : (1) A Mutawalli has power to grant a lease of Waqf property, if it is agricultural land for a term not exceeding three years, and if non-agricultural land for a term not exceeding one year. If the term of the period exceeds, he has to obtain the permission and authorisation from the Waqf Board. (Sec. 36-B) Waqf Act-1954.

(2) A Mutawalli has no power, without the permission of the court, to mortgage, sell or exchange or any other alienation of the Waqf property. (Sec. 36-A).

(3) Mutawalli has the powers to alienate the Waqf property under the genuine circumstances, with the permission of court.

(4) Mutawalli has to the powers to remove of encroachments from Waqf property with the help of Waqf commissioner.

(5) Every Mutawalli has the power to protect the Waqf property and shall use all precautionary, appropriate and genuine steps as per the customs and Acts.

(6) Every Mutawalli shall prepare statement of Accounts of Income and Expenses of Waqf property and to submit copies to the Commissioner of Waqf Board.

(b) Duties of Mutawalli (Section 50 of Waqf Act 1995)

(1) Every Mutawalli shall have to carry out the directions made by the Board or Waqf Commissioner.

(2) he has to discharge the public dues.

(3) He has to do any other act which he is lawfully required to do by or under Waqf Act

(4) He has to register the Waqf, if not registered.

(5) He has to allow the inspection of Waqf, properties, accounts, records or deeds and documents relating there to by any officer of Waqf Board or Waqf Commissioner, etc.

Question No. 40

Write a short note on Pre-Emption (Shuffa).

Answer :

The Arabic word of Pre-Emption is 'Shufa', which means conjunction. It is a right to take possession of property sold to another by paying a price similar to that settled or paid by the purchaser. The person entitled to claim pre-emption is called "Shafo" or Pre-Emptor".

Definition :

The word 'pre-emption' is derived from 'prae emptio' a Latin word which means the act of buying before another, the act of right of purchasing before others. 'Pre-emption' means 'the right of first buying of a thing'.

The technical Arabic rterm for its Anglo-Mohammedan equivalent 'pre-emption' is *Shufaa'*. *'Shufaa'* literally means 'adding'. In law, Shufaa is to acquire an immovable property by force exercised against the purchaser thereof, in lieu of what the latter had to pay for the same. In law, pre-emption means 'a right which the owner of certain immovable property possesses, as such, for the quiet enjoyment of that immovable property, to obtain in substitution for the buyer, proprietary ossession of certain other immovable property, not his own, on such terms as those on which such latter immovable property is sold to another person'.

The person entitled to claim the right is called the 'shafi' or the pre-emptor. When the contract for the sale of immovable property is made, he claims to occupy the place or the buyer in order to take the property at the same price and on the same conditions as it has been agreed upon.

According to Mulla, "The right of pre-emption or shufaa is a right which the owenr of an imoable property possesses to acquire bypurcfhase another immovable property which has ben sold to another person."

Mahomed Ullah ibn S. Jung says, " 'Shufaa' means a right to acquire by compulsory purchase some immovable property in preference to all other persons by reason of such right."

In *Govind Dayal vs. Inayatullah,* [7 All. (1885) 779] Mahmood, J. defined pre-emption as "a right which the owner of certain immovable property possesses, as such, for the quiet enjoyment of that immovbable property, to obtain, in substitution for the buyr, proprietary ossession of certain toher immovable property not his own, on such terms as those on wyhich such latter immovable property is sold to another person.

Wilson defines pre-emption as a right to acquire by compulsory purchase, in certain cases, immobable property in preference to all other persons.

The House of Lords in *Dickinson vs. Dodes,* [(1876) 2 Ch. 463] defined pre-emption as "An option to purchase within a given time, or at any time, without reference to any intended sale to a third party, is included under the same name."

Sweet Law Dictionary provides that "The right of pre-emption is the right of purchasing property before or in preference to other persons."

According to Tomlins Law Dictionary, pre-emption is "The right of first buying of a thing".

Objects of Pre-Emption :

Rights of pre-emption have been created by contract between the sharers in a village. In all cases the object is as far as possible to prevent strangers to a village from becoming sharers in the village, likely to cause both inconvenience and vexation.

The rule of pre-emption aims at the checking of the difficulties and inconvenience which may result to families and communities from the appearance of a stranger as a coparcener or near neighbour. The object of the law of pre-emption is to enable landowners to avoid the advent of an undersirable neigbour.

Pre-emption tends to advent division which other would cause loss and damages.

In *Enatullah vs. Sheikh Kowsher Ali,* [AIR 1926 Cal. 1153], it was observed that the doctrine of pre-emption as it is at presentg accepted, does o appear to be based entirely on the ground of preveing a disagreeable stranger from coming in, but it is on a conjuctin with the lands sold that they

Subject of Pre-Emption : It is reported that the Prophet had said that there was no *shufaa* (pre-emption) except in a house or a garden. Hence, the Mohammedan law lays down that landed property (immovable property) alohne, including houses and gardens, can be subject to the law of pre-emption. If the property consists of a share in a village or a large estate, a mere neighbour cannot claim pre-emption; but a co-sharer can, and probably also a participator in appendages.

The right of the pre-emption applies only to aqar (immovable property) whether divisible or not. Like the right of an easement, it is a right annexed to land under Muslim law. It takes effect with regard to property sold, or parted with by any other mode which is equivalent to sale. Aqar is wide term which may include all fixtures which are permanently attached to land, thus it cannot be confined to land only. Aqar, thus, includes fixtures on land such as buildings, trees or mills etc.

In Shafii law property which is incapable of division cannot be the subject of pre-emption.

Some Shia authorities allow the right of pre-emption to be exercised even in cases of movable properties under the expression 'aqar'.

Requirements of Pre-Emption : (i) The pre-emptor should be a Muslim;

(ii) He should be the owner of certain property;

(iii) The right of pre-emption arises only when some other owner has sold property;

(iv) The buyer need not be a Mohammedan.

(v) The necessary demand for pre-emption should be made.

Legal Effects of pre-emption :—

The following are the Legal effects of pre-emption :—

(1) When the claim of pre-emption is complete, the pre-emptor steps in the shoes of buyer.

(2) If the sale has been completed when the claim to the right of pre-emption is enforced, the original buyer becomes the new seller, and the pre-emptor as the new buyer.

(3) The pre-emptor does not become liable for any contingent charges incurred by the buyer, such as brokerage or agency.

(4) The buyer is entitled to receive or retain the rents and profits of the land during the interval between the date of its sale to himself, and its transfer to the pre-emptor.

(5) As the pre-emptor takes the property from the buyer and not the seller, the buyer must always be a party to the suit.

(6) If before the sale is complete and the pre-emptor claims if from the buyer, he may say to the pre-emptor to take it direct from the seller.

UNIT -- V

INHERITANCE AND SUCCESSION

Question No. 41

Write a note on Inheritance under Muslim Law ?

Answer :

The Islamic Law of inheritance is a combination of the pre-Islamic customs and the rules introduced by the Prophet. Whatever is left after the death of a Muslim is his heritable property. This property can be movable or immovable and ancestral or self-acquired. The estate of a deceased Muslim devolves on his heirs separately and the heirs are entitled to hold the property as tenants-in-common, each having a definite share in the property.

In *Abdul Raheem vs. Land Acquisition Officer,* AIR 1989 A.P. 318, it was held that the joint system family or joint property is unknown to Muslim law and therefore the right, title and interest in the land held by the person stands extinguished and stands vested in other persons.

RULES OF INHERITANCE OF PROPERTY

The general rule of inheritance states that the inheritance opens on the death of the person. Nobody can claim any right in the property even if he is an heir.

Birth right :--Any child born into a Muslim family does not get his right to property on his birth. In fact, no such person becomes a legal heir and therefore holds no right till the time of the death of the ancestor. If an heir lives even after the death of the ancestor, he becomes a legal heir and is therefore entitled to a share in property. However, if the apparent heir does not survive his ancestor, then no such right of inheritance or share in the property shall exist.

Rule of Representation : Doctrine of representation states that if during the lifetime of an ancestor, any of his or her legal heirs die, but the latter's heirs still survive, then such heirs shall become entitled to a share in the property as now they shall be representing their immediate generation.

Doctrine of Representation finds its recognition in the Roman, English and Hindu laws of inheritance. However, this doctrine of representation does not find its place in the Muslim law of inheritance.

Rule of Distribution : Vesting of property takes place immediately on the death of the propositus. Under the Muslim law, distribution of property can be made in two ways, firstly per capita or per strip distribution. Per - Capita distribution method is majorly used in the Sunni law. According to this method, the estate left over by the ancestors gets equally distributed among the heirs. Therefore, the share of each person depends on the number of heirs. The heir does not represent the branch from which he inherits.

On the other hand, per strip distribution method is recognised in the Shia law. According to this method of property inheritance, the property gets distributed among the heirs according to the strip they belong to. Hence the quantum of their inheritance also depends upon the branch and the number of persons that belong to the branch. It is noteworthy that the Shia law recognises the principle of representation for a limited purpose of calculating the extent of the share of each person. Moreover, under the

Shia law, this rule is applicable for determining the quantum of the share of the descendants of a pre-deceased daughter, pre-deceased brother, pre-deceased sister or that of a pre-deceased aunt.

Grounds of Disqualifications :--Disqualifications which debar the heirs to succeed the property of the intestate are—

Murderer :--Under the Sunni Law, a person who has caused the death of another, whether intentionally, or by mistake, negligence, or accident, is debarred from succeeding to the estate of that other.

Homicide under the Shia Law is not a bar to succession unless the death was caused intentionally.

Illegitimate Children :--Under the Hanafi School, an illegitimate child is not entitled to inherit. Such a child cannot inherit from his/her father but can inherit from his/her mother and all relatives of the mother. The mother can also inherit the property of her illegitimate children.

Widow :--Under Muslim law, no widow is excluded from the succession. A childless Muslim widow is entitled to one-fourth of the property of the deceased husband, after meeting his funeral and legal expenses and debts. However, a widow who has children or grandchildren is entitled to one-eighth of the deceased husband's property.

In Abdul Hammed Khan vs. Peare Mirza, 1935 I.L.R. 10 Luck. 550 it was held that a childless widow, in the absence of other heirs, was entitled to inherit her share and rest of the property including the land, of her husband by the application of the doctrine of return.

Child in the Womb :--A child in the womb of its mother is competent to inherit only if it is born alive. A child in embryo is regarded as a living person and, as such, the property vests immediately in that child. But, if such a child in the womb is not born alive, the share already vested in it is divested and, it is presumed as if there was no such heir (in the womb) at all.

Escheat :--Where a deceased Muslim has no legal heir under Muslim law, his properties are inherited by Government through the process of escheat.

Difference of Religion :--A non-Muslim could not inherit from a Muslim but the Caste Disabilities Removal Act of 1850 does away in India with the exclusion of a non-Muslim from the inheritance of the property.

Theory of Propinquity :--Propinquity means nearness in blood. In determining the preferential claims of the heirs, the Shias adopt the principles of consanguinity. The rule that nearer in degree excludes the more remote is applied to kindred of the same class only. This theory of propinquity is fully recognized by Shias but partially recognized by the Sunnis.

Case Laws

1. In *Hakim Rehman vs. Mohammad Mahmood Hassan*, AIR 1957 Pat 559, it was held that upon the death of a Mohammedan, the whole estate devolves upon his heirs at the moment of his death and the heirs succeed to the estate as tenants-in-common in specific shares.

2. In *Rukmanibai vs. Bismillavai*, AIR 1993 MP 45, it was held that where a person, who has converted to Islam, dies leaving behind his daughter only and no residuary, shall be

entitled to her share as well as residuary share in the property of the deceased.

3. In *Shukurllah vs. Zohra Bibi*, AIR 1932 All. 512 it was held that each heir of the Mohammedan is liable for the debt of the deceased to the extent only of a share of the debts proportionate to his share of the estate.

Question No. 42

What are the rules regarding administration of the estate of the deceased ?

Answer :

According to the provisions of the Indian Succession Act which prevails even if they come in conflict with Muslim Law the estate of the deceased Muslim is directed to be applied for the satisfaction of the claims in the following order viz.

(1) Defraying the reasonable funeral expenses and death-bed charges, including fees for medical attendance and board and lodging for one month previous to his death.

(2) The expenses of obtaining probate and Letters of Administration or succession or certificate and other certificate and other expenses on judicial proceedings necessary in the administration of the estate.

(3) The wages of any domestic servant, labourer or artisan for services rendered to the deceased within three (3) months next preceding his death.

(4) Other debts of the deceased according to their respective priorities, if any.

(5) Legacies not exceeding one-third of what remains after all the above payments have been made.

(6) Duty upon the estate of the deceased under the Estate Duty Act where it is leviable upon the estate.

(7) The distribution of the residue among the heirs of the deceased will take place according to the law of sect to which he belonged at the time of his death.

(8) The right of an heir to alienate his own share is not affected by the non-payment of dower debt.

Vesting of Estate :—In the case of a Muslim who dies intestate his entire estate vests in the following manner :

(a) Administrator : If the Muslim dies intestate his entire estate vests in the administrator to whom letters of Administration are granted by the court. The Administrator appointed must not be minor or of unsound mind.

(b) Executor : When the deceased leaves a will, his property vests in the Executor, who becomes the legal representative of the deceased for all matters. The Executor after the realisation of the estate is a bare trustee for the heirs as to non-bequeathable two-thirds and an active trustee as to one-third for the purposes of the will.

Question No. 43

Discuss the Special features of Muslim Law of Inheritance and bring out the main differences between Sunni (Hanafi) Law and Shia Law ?

Answer :

Special Features of Inheritance

(1) Under Sunni (Hanafi) and Shia Laws, no distinction between movable and immovable property or between ancestral, self-acquired or separate property.

(2) Under Shia Law, a childless widow is not entitled to a share in the land belonging to her husband.

(3) Under Shia Law the eldest son, if he is of sound-mind, is entitled to succeed exclusively to the wearing appeal of the father and to his Koran, sword and ring.

(4) No one can have any share in the inheritance of another till after his death.

(5) Under Sunni Law, the right of representation is not recognised. But under Shia law, it is recognised to the limited degree.

(6) The chance of a Muslim heir-apparent succeeding to an estate cannot be the subject of a valid transfer or release.

(7) An apostate from Islam whether a male or female is excluded from inheritance to any one, whether a Muslim or an apostate according to Muslim Law.

(8) An illegitimate is considered to be the son of his mother only. There are mutual rights of inheritance only with the mother and maternal relations. But under Shia law he has no such right.

(9) The spouse, the descendants, the mother and the maternal relations but the father, shall have mutual rights of inheritance with an illegitimate person.

Distinction between Sunni (Hanafi) and Shia Laws of Inheritance ?

	Sunni Law of Inheritance	Shia Law of Inheritance
1. Classification of heirs	i. The classification of heirs under Sunni Law is rather unnatural	The classification of heirs under Shia law is more natural.
	ii. There are three classes of heirs :	ii. There are two groups of heirs :
	a. Shares	a. Sharers, and
	b. Residuaries; and	b. Residuaries
	c. Distant Kindred.	There is no class of distant kindred as such under Shia Law.
	iii. Sharers exclude residuaries; residuaries exclude distant kindred	iii. Sharers and residuaries are together divided into three classes in a particular order of preference.
	iv. Under Sunni Law, the distant kind-	iv. Under Shia Law, the distant kind-

	red are postponed to sharers and residuaries.	red inherit alongwith sharers and residuaries.
	v. Sunnis prefer agnates to cognates.	v. Shias prefer the nearest Kinsman, whether he is an agnate or cognate.
2. Rule of premogeniture	The Sunni Law does not recognise the doctgrine of 'Premogeniture' (*i.e.* first born)	The Shia Law recognises the doctrine of premogeniture. Thus, the eldest son is entitled to his deceased father's sword, wearing apparel and Quran.
3. Principle of Consanguinity	The principle of consanguinity is not recognised in Sunni Law. The Sunnis prefer agnates to cognates.	The Shia Law adopts the Principle of consanguinity and not of agnacy. the Shias prefer the nearest kinsmen whether they are agnates or cognates.
		They do not recognise any separate class of heirs corresponding to the distant kindred of the Sunni Law. All heirs under the Shia

		Law are either sharers or residuaries.
4. Doctrine of Representation	Doctrine of Representation is not recognised	The Doctrine of Representation is the key-note of the whole system of the Shia Law of inheritance. Doctrine of Representation gives two meanings; (i) Determination of heirs, what persons are entitled to inherit from the deceased; and (ii) Determination of the quantum of the share what he is entitled to inherit.
5. Kind of property	There is no distinction between movable and immovable property left by the deceased in Sunni Law	In the case of a childless widow, she is not allowed to take any share in her husband's immovable property.
6. Doctrine of Aul (increase)	Under Sunni Law the doctrine of 'increase'	Under Shia Law, the doctgrine of 'increase'

	extends to all the sharers	applies only against the daughter and sister.
7. Doctrine of *Radd* (Return)	Under the Sunni Law all the sharers, except the husband or wife share in the return and even the husband or wife gets the residue on the total failure of other heirs.	Under the Shia Law, the wife can never get benefit by the return and the mother and uterine brother and sister are excluded from the share under certain conditions.
8. Devolution of the residue	If the deceased leaves behind a single daughter and father according to the Sunnis, the residue goes to the father.	According to Shias, the residue is divided amongst the sharers by return.
9. Illegitimate child	Illegitimate child is entitled to inherit the properties of the mother. But he is not entitled to inherit the properties of father.	Illegitimate child is not entitled to inherit either from the father or from the mother.
10. Disqualification of murderer	In Sunni School of Law, the murderer is excluded from the inheritance, whether he intentionally or accidentally, murders	The Shia School excludes the murderer from the inheritance if he has intentionally causes the murder of the person

	of the person from whom he is going to inherit.	from whom he is going to inherit.
11. Sharers and their shares	i. The Sunnis do not interfere with the Quranic sharers except that, on the authority of the ijma and qiyas, they introduce into the list of sharers, the true grand-father, the true grand-mother and the son's daughter. ii. There are twelve sharers iii. Husband (wife) : Sharers are reduced only by child or child of a son. iv. Father : a. may suceed both as sharer	i. The Shias keep the Quranic list intact but re-arrange it in a group division on the basis of 'propinquity'. ii. There are nine sharers. iii. Husband (wife) : Their shares are reduced by all lineal descendants whether son's or through daughter's. iv. Father : a. only as sharer or as residuary.

	and as residuary at one time.	
	b. becomes residuary when there is no son or child of son	b. becomes residuary when there is no lineal descendant.
	v. Mother :	v. Mother :
	a. Share is 1/6 or 1/3 of residue after deducting share of spouse.	a. Share is either 1/6 or 1/3
	b. Share is reduced by child or child of son.	b. Share is reduced by all lineal descendants.
	vi. Uterine brothers and sisters: They are excluded by child or child of son, father or true grand-father	vi. Uterine brothers and sisters : Excluded by parents and all lineal descendants.
	vii. Full and Consanguine sisters :	vii. Full and Consanguine sisters :
	a. excluded by child, child of	a. excluded by parents and all

	son, father and true grand-father.	lineal descendants.
	b. they become residuries with a brother or when there are daughters or son's daughters.	b. they become residuaries with a brother and also with paternal grandfather.
	viii. True grand father, true grandmother and son's daughers : These are sharers.	viii. True grand father, true grandmother and son's daughtrs : These are not sharers at all.

Question No. 44

Explain the Doctrine of Aul and Rudd in Muslim Law?

Answer :

Doctrine of Aul (Increase) :--When the inheritance is distributed among the Koranic sharers, sometimes the total exceeds Unity. This cannot be for the entire estate is one unit only. So the share allottable to each sharer is proportionately reduced. The formula adopted for this purpose is to bring all the fractional sharers to one common denominator. Then the denominator of each share is increased so as to be equal to the sum of the numerators. By this increasing the denominator, the fractional shares are all proportionately reduced. This is called the Doctrine of Aul or Doctrine of Increase.

Difference between Shia and Sunni Law of 'Increase':

According to the Sunni law, the doctrine implies proportionate reduction of all the shares. According to the Shia law, on the other hand, it implies the reduction of the shares of the daughter or the daughter and full or consanguine sister or sisters only. Other heirs do not suffer.

Illustrative Examples:

The following are a few illustrative examples of the application of the Doctrine of Increase:

(a) Husband 1/2 = 3/6 reduced to 3/8

2 Full sisters 2/3 = 4/6 reduced to 4/8
Mother 1/6 = 1/6 reduced to 1/8
Total: 8/6 8/8

(b) Husband 1/4 = 3/12 reduced to 3/13
Mother 1/6 = 2/12 reduced to 2/13
2 Daughters 2/3 = 8/12 reduced to 8/13
Total: 13/12 13/13

(c) Widow 1/4 = 3/12 reduced to 3/13
Mother 1/3 = 4/12 reduced to 4/13
Full sister 1/2 = 6/12 reduced to 6/13
Total: 13/12 13/13

(d) Husband 1/4 = 3/12 reduced to 3/15
Father 1/6 = 2/12 reduced to 2/15
Mother 1/6 = 2/12 reduced to 2/15
3 Daughters ... 2/3 = 8/12 reduced to 8/15
Total: 15/12 15/15

Doctrine of Rudd (Return) : Sometimes when the inheritance is distributed among the sharers, the total of the shares is less than unity. The remainder should go to the Residuaries. But there may be no residuaries among the relations of the propositus. In such a case the residue returns to the sharers themselves and their shares are proportionately increased. The formula adopted when there is no husband (or wife) among sharers, is to reduce the shares to a common denominator and then the denominator of each share is reduced so as to be equal to the sum of the numerators. By this reducing the denominator the fractional shares are proportionately increased. This is called the Doctrine of Rudd or Doctrine of Return.

Shia Law :

Under the Shia law, if there is a surplus after satisfying the shares, it is not necessary that there should be no residuaries in order to apply the doctrine of return. If there is a surplus left after the allotment of shares of the sharers, but there are no residuaries in the class to which the shares belong, the surplus reverts to the sharers in the proportion of their respective shares.

Difference between 'Increase' and 'Return':

The doctrine of "return" is the converse of the doctrine of "increase". In "increase", the shares exceed unity, and suffer a proportionate reduction. In "return", the shares fall short of unity, and are proportionately increased. In return, the husband and wife do not benefit if there is any other sharer or a distant kindred, but they are not saved from the operation of the doctrine of increase.

Thus, the important points of difference between the two are as under:

1. In 'Increase', the total of the shares adds up to more than unity; whereas in 'return' the total falls short of unity.

2. In 'Increase', the shares undergo rateable reduction. In 'Return', the shares undergo a rateable increase.

3. In 'Increase', the share of the husband or wife suffers a proportionate reduction along with other sharers. In 'Return', the husband or wife is not entitled to the 'Return' so long as there is any other heir, whether sharer or distant kindred.

Question No. 45

What are the Differences between the Muslim and Hindu Law of Inheritance and Succession ?

Answer :

Muslim Law of Inheritance	Hindu Law of Inheritance
1. Muslim Law does not recognise survivorship.	Hindu Law recognise survivorship which is an incident of a coparcenary governed by the Mitakshara Law.
2. Muslim Law makes no difference between the ancestral and self-acquired property for purposes of inheritance	The Hindu Law differenciates the ancestral and self-acquired property for purposes of inheritance.
3. The Sunni Law does not recognised the Right of Representation	The Hindu Law recognises the Right of Representation in the case of sons, grandsons and great-grand-sons.
4. The rule of a male getting double the share of a female of the same degree is peculiar to the Mohammedan Law	The Share of a female in the property is unknown n ancient Hindu Law. (Mitakshara) but allowed equal share under Hindu Succession Act, 1956.
5. Under the Mohammedan Law female's right to inherit property is absolute with full powers of disposal like any other male heir.	Under the Orthodox Hindu Law the female got a life estate in most cases. The law has since been modified by the Hindu Succession Act, 1956.

6.	Under Mohammedan Law, a son does not exclude father, mother, and daughter	Under the Orthodox Hindu Law a son excludes father, mother and daugher. Under the Hindu Succession Act, 1956, the conditions are changed.
7.	Under the Mohammedan Law females are not excluded by males but succeeded with them.	Formerly in Hindu Law males generally excluded females. This is not now under the Hindu Succession Act, 1956.
8.	Under the Mohammedan Law tghe heirship is determined on the basis of Nasab, Sabab, and wala.	Under Mitakshara law, consanguinity or blood relationship and on the basis of capacity to confer spiritual bene4fits also.
9.	Under the Muslim Law, unchastity is not a ground for exclusion from inheritance.	Under the Hindu Law unchastity of the wife disqualifies her from inheritance.
10.	Among Shias a female does not inherit from her illegitimate sons.	Among Hindus, a female does inherit from her illegitimate sons.

Question No. 46

Given in brief the object and scope of the Indian Succession Act, 1925. To whom does it apply?

Answer :

The Indian Succession Act, 1925 broadly deals with the two categories of succession, viz. testamentary succession and intestate succession. In a case where there is a written will testamentary succession is applicable. On the other hand, when there is no will and the properties of the deceased need to be distributed as per the religious laws, intestate succession is applicable.

Object of the Act : The Indian Succession Act as enacted in Act No. XXXIX of 1925 is purely a considering measure. It does not affect the rights of coparcershipas between those to whom it applies, nor does it purport to enlarge the category of heritable property. (AIR 193 Bom. 25).

Scope of the Act : The provisions of the Indian Succession Act, 1925 regulate intestate as well as testamentary succession.

Part X of the Act, containing rules of intestate succession, do not apply to any intestacy occurring before the first day of January 1866 Part X also does not apply to the property of any Christian, Muslim, Hindu, Sikh, Buddhist or Jain. But the Act does not prohibit a Hindu from succeeding to the property of a Christian. Thus, a Hindu father can succeed to his Christian son, who was originally a Hindu but afterwards adopted Christianity. (*Administrator General vs. Ananda Chari,* Mad. 466 471). Similarly, Hindu brothers and sisters can succeed to the property of their deceased brother who had become a Christian. (*Nepbuala vs. Sittikanta,* 15 C.W.N. 158).

To whom applicable : This Act applies to the following persons:

1. Europeans by birth and descent having the Indian domicile.
2. Persons of mixed European and Indian blood, Indian Christians except as provided by the Act, East Indians, Jews and Armanians.
3. Parsis as specifically provided in the Act.
4. Converts to christianity.
5. Hindus and Muslims only so far as the provisions in the Act are not in conflict with their respective laws.

Succession for Hindus : In the case of Hindus, the laws relating to the testamentary succession are applicable as per the Indian Succession Act, 1925. However, the laws relating to the intestate succession are applicable as per the Hindu Succession Act, 1956.

In the case of intestate succession for Hindus, the Indian Succession Act, 1925 is not applicable due to the existence of the system of Hindu Undivided Family or HUF as per the Hindu Law. Thus, the Hindu Succession Act, 1956 came into existence in order to deal with the succession as per the Hindu law and culture.

Succession for Muslims : In the case of Muslims, the Indian Succession Act, 1925 is not applicable to both the testamentary and intestate succession. In their case, the succession is on the basis of the Quran and other sources.

Hedaya or FatawaAlamgiri is the guiding authority on the subject of wills for Muslims. As per the Muslim Law, the properties of the deceased shall be applied in the payment of the following and in the order below:

1. Funeral and death bed charges.
2. Probate or letters of administration or succession certificate expenses.
3. Payment of any wages due for any services to any laborer, artisan or domestic servant for rendering of services to the deceased within 3 months just preceding his death.
4. Payment of any other debts of the deceased.
5. Legacies to a maximum of one-third of what remains after all the above payments
6. The remaining two-thirds shall go to heirs as on intestacy.

Succession for Sikhs : The Indian Succession Act, 1925 is applicable to laws relating to the testamentary succession in the case of Sikhs. However, in the case of intestate succession of Sikhs the Hindu Succession Act, 1956 is applicable.

Christian Succession Act : In the case of Christians the laws of Indian Succession Act, 1925 is applicable to both testamentary and intestate succession.

Succession for Jains : The Indian Succession Act includes Jains and treats them as Hindus. Thus, the provisions applicable to the Hindus are also applicable to the Jains. The testamentary succession laws are applicable as per the Indian Succession Act, 1925 while the intestate succession laws are applicable as per the Hindu Succession Act, 1956 to the Jains.

Succession for Buddhists : The testamentary succession laws are applicable as per the Indian Succession Act, 1925 while the intestate succession laws are applicable as per the Hindu Succession Act, 1956 to the Buddhists.

Question No. 47

Write a note on Succession in Respect of Christians?

Answer :

The Indian Succession Act, 1925 provides for the inheritance laws for all other religions, including Christians. Christians have varied laws on succession and familial relations. The rules for succession among the Christians has been codified under the Indian Succession Act, 1925, while on the other hand customary practices also have an influence on the principles of inheritance. The British Indian Government enacted the Indian Succession Act, 1865 which was to apply in the case of Christians. This Act was later replaced by the Indian Succession Act, 1925, which currently governs the inheritance in case of Christians. Certain customary practices also influence the principles of inheritance in case of Christians and have also been considered by the courts in India.

This Act recognizes three types of heirs for Christians:-

1. **Spouse**

2. **Lineal Descendants :** The phrase "Lineal Descendant" means, "a Descendant born out of a lawful marriage". Thus a daughter's illegitimate son or a son's illegitimate daughter or other illegitimate issue cannot be said to be a "Lineal Descendant". An illegitimate child is not a child within the meaning of the act. Therefore, such a child has no share in the property of the parents. But in *Jane Anthony vs. Siyath,* 2008 (4) KLT 1002 recognized the right of illegitimate child under Indian Succession Act.

3. **Kindred :** The term "Kindred" means, relations by blood through a lawful marriage.Therefore, relations by illegitimate birth are not recognized as Kindred under the Act. Kindred does not include relation by affinity such as mother-in-law or step mother or step father. Thus, a step father or a step mother has no legal right of Succession to the property of his or her step children. The position is the same in the case of a father-in-law as well.

The Concept of Succession : Section 2(d) of the Act defines "Indian Christian" means, a native of India who is or in good faith claims to be, of unmixed Asiatic Descent and who professes any form of the Christian Religion. The religion of the deceased determines the Succession to his estate. Succession, in brief, deals with how the property of a deceased person devolves on his heirs. This property may be ancestral or self acquired and may devolve in two ways.

1. By Testamentary Succession *i.e.,* when the deceased has left a will bequeathing his property to specific heirs.

2. By Intestate Succession, when the deceased has not left a will whereby the law governing the deceased (according to his religion) steps in, and determines how his estate will devolve.

Testamentary Succession among Indian Christians : A will is the expression by a person of wishes which he intends to take effect only at his death. In order to make a valid will, a testator must have a testamentary intention to which he gives deliberate expression to take effect only at his death.

Testamentary Succession is dealt with under Part VI of Indian Succession Act, 1925. Part VI of the Act has Sections 57 to

191, that comprehensively deal with all issues connected with wills and codicils and the making and enforcing of the same, capacity and formalities to make a will. According to Section 59, every person of sound mind, not being a minor may dispose of his property by will. Married women, deaf/dumb/ blind persons who are not there by incapacitated to make a will are all entitled to disposing their property by will. Soundness of mind and freedom from intoxication or any illness that render a person incapable of knowing what he is doing are laid down as pre-requisites to the process.

Intestate Succession among Indian Christians : Section 30 of the Indian Succession Act, 1925 defines Intestate Succession thus, a person is deemed to die intestate in respect of all property of which he has not made a testamentary dispossession which is capable of taking effect. Thus, any property which has not already been bequeathed or allocated as per legal process, will, upon the death of the owner, in so far, as he is an Indian Christian, devolve as per the Rules contained in Chapter II of the Act. If a person has not made a testamentary disposition of his property which is capable of taking effect, he is deemed to have died intestate in respect of his entire estate. Intestacy is either total or partial. There is a total intestacy where thedeceased does not effectively dispose of any beneficial interest in any of his property by will. There is a partial intestacy where the deceased effectively dispossess of some, but not all, of the beneficial interest in his property by will.

UNIT -- VI

OTHER PERSONAL LAWS

Question No. 48

Describe the salient features of the Special Marriage Act, 1954 ?

Answer :

The Special Marriage Act deals with inter-caste and inter-religion marriages. Inter caste marriage is a marriage between people of two different castes.

In 1872, **H.S. Maine** introduced **Act III of 1872**, which gave permission to dissenters to marry whoever they choose under new Civil Marriage Law. But it was inadequate. In 1954 Parliament enacted ***Special Marriage Act, 1954*** to provide for registration and validation of special form of marriage in India.

The new enactment has three major objectives:

1. To provide for the special form of marriage in certain cases;
2. To provide for the registration of certain marriages; and
3. To provide for Divorce.

Scope of Special Marriage Act :--Inter-caste marriages are those marriages where bride and groom, both are from different caste and religion. Earlier in India, marrying in other caste considered a crime against the community.

However, Inter-caste marriages have gained acceptance due to improvement in the lifestyle and upbringing of people. Today's generation is trying to break-free the ties of orthodoxy and prefer to choose their partner themselves irrespective of their caste. For the acceptance of such marriage, our Parliament enacted a proper legislation *i.e.* Special Marriage Act. It gave condition and requirement for the special marriage. Also in the case of mishappening, it gave power to courts to interfere.

Application of the Act :--Chapter 1 of The Special Marriage Act deals with the applicability of the act.

. These acts cover all the religions namely, Hindu, Muslim, Sikhs, Christians, Jews, Buddhists.

. It also applies not only to the people living in India but also to the Indian nationals living abroad.

Essentials / Conditions for Marriage :--Chapter 2: Solemnization of Marriage' has laid down certain conditions to be fulfilled strictly. If not followed, marriage will be considered as Void Ab Initio.The conditions or essentials required for a marriage under the Special Marriage Act are as follows:—

(1) Neither party should have a husband or wife living;

(2) Neither party is an idiot or lunatic;

(3) The bridegroom must have completed the age of 21 years and the bride the age of 18 years.

(4) The parties are not within the degree of prohibited relationship which are numerated in the first schedule of the Act;

(5) Where the marriage is solemnized outside the territories to which the Act applies, both parties should be citizens of the domiciled within the territories to which the Act applies.

Provision for Divorce :--Special Marriage Act prohibits the filing of divorce petition within one year of marriage. Moreover, in case the court has reason to believe that the petitioner had to experience hardships or the respondent has failed to provide the basics. In that case, the court can entertain the petition. And if the court finds some misrepresentation on the part of the petitioner, the court can deny to maintain the petition and will entertain the same after the expiration of one year.

Grounds for divorce under this Act: Section 27

Parties may belong to different religions when they perform a marriage under this Act, but they will have similar ground for getting a divorce, as mentioned below:

- Adultery.
- Desertion: Respondent has deserted the petitioner for a continuous period of not less than two years.
- Respondent being sentenced to imprisonment for seven years or more for any offence.
- Cruelty
- Respondent has been incurably of unsound mind.
- Respondent has been suffering from venereal disease.

- Respondent has been suffering from an incurable form of leprosy.
- Presumption of death: Respondent not heard of as being alive for more than seven years.
- The respondent-husband has been convicted of crimes such as rape or outraging the modesty of any female.
- The wife may also get a divorce on the ground that there was no resumption of cohabitation for one year or more since the passing of decree or order for maintenance.

Question No. 49

What are the grounds of Divorce provided by the Special Marriage Act 1954 ?

Answer :

Divorce is a process by which the marriage is dissolved. after dissolution of the marriage, (Divorce) parties revert to their are unmarried status and are free to marry again.

(1) Grounds of Divorce (Section 27 of Special Marriage Act, 1954)

Either husband or wife can file a petition for divorce to the district court on the ground that the respondent-

(1) Has, after the solemnization of the marriage. had voluntary sexual intercourse with any person other than his or her spouse, or

(2) Has deserted the petitioner for a continuous period of not less than two years immediately preceding the presentation of the petition; or

(3) If undergoing a sentence of imprisonment for seven years or more for an offence as defined in the Indian Penal Code;

(4) Has since the solemnization of the marriage treated the petitioner with cruelty; or

(5) Has been incurably of unsound mind, or hits been suffering continuously or intermittently from mental disorder of such a kind and to such all extent that the petitioner cannot reasonably be expected to live with the respondent.

(6) Has been suffering from venereal disease in a communicable form; or

(7) Has been suffering from leprosy, the disease not having been contracted from the petitioner; or,

(8) Has not been heard of as being alive for period of seven years or more by those persons who would naturally have heard of the respondent if the respondent had been alive;

(9) Has not a resumed cohabitation for one year or more after the passing of a decree for judicial separation against respondent;

(10) has failed to comply with a decree for restitution of conjugal rights for one year or more.

(2) Special grounds for wife :--A wife may also present a petition for divorce to the district court on the ground,–

(i) That her husband has, since the solemnization of the marriage, been guilty of rape, sodomy or bestiality;

(ii) though order for separate maintenance was passed against husband, he has not the resumed cohabitation for one year or upwards.

Under Special Marriage Act, 1954 Divorce is possible by Mutual Consent. If the husband and wife are living separately for one year or more than one year and are not able to live together then they may mutually agree that the marriage should be dissolved. A petition for divorce may be presented by both the parties stating this facts.

Question No. 50

Write a short note on The Indian Divorce Act 1869?

Answer :

The Indian Divorce Act governs divorce among the Christian couples in India. Divorce is the legal dissolution of the marital union between a man and a woman. According to this act, the separation is granted by the court of law after receiving a petition from either wife or husband. Divorce is followed by granting alimony, child custody, and child visitation, distribution of property and distribution of debts

Section 2 of the Indian Divorce Act, 1869 provides that so far as a suit for dissolution is concerned, the parties to the marriage must be domiciled in India at the time of presentation of the petition. If the husband has Indian domicile, the condition is fulfilled, because after marriage the wife acquires the domicile of the husband. (*Aattaullah vs. Attaullah,* AIR 1953 Cal. 350).

Section 3 of the Act deals with professes the Christian religion. The Indian Divorce Act applies to Christians. The petitioner or the respondent must be a Christian. It is not necessary for both the parties to profess the Christian religion; it is sufficient for one party to be a Christian. (*Sasivarnam vs. Gnana Sundari,* ILR 1954 Mad. 737).

Nowhere in the Divorce Act is it required that the marriage in respect of which relief is sought, should have been solemnized in any particular form. It is sufficient that one of the Parsis is a Christian when the petition is filed. (*Mrs. Ramila Khosla vs. Rajnish Khosla,* AIR 1979 Del. 78).

Section 3 (9) of the Indian Divorce Act, 1869 as implying an abandonment against the wish of the person charging it, is called Desertion. Leaving the matrimonial home by consent or separate living by mutual consent, express or tacit is not desertion within the meaning of this law. Desertion in order to be a ground for a divorce under the last clause of section 10 of the Indian Divorce Act must be desertion without reasonable excuse. In other words, if desertion is with a reasonable excuse it cannot be a ground of divorce under that section. It is observed in the case of *Kanal Lal Majumdar vs. Rama Majumdar,* 1988 (1) HLP 118 (Cal.).

Grounds for Dissolution of Marriage : Section 10 of the Indian Divorce Act contains grounds on which a court may dissolve a marriage. In order to avail a divorce, the husband or wife must file a petition before the District Court. This is basically the court under whose jurisdiction the parties solemnized their marriage or they reside or last resided together.

The court may grant a divorce under any of the following grounds:

(a) When one of the parties commits adultery;

(b) If a party ceases to be a Christian;

(c) In case of a party being of unsound mind for two years;

(d) If a party has been suffering from leprosy or a venereal disease for two years;

(e) In case of a party wilfully refusing to consummate the marriage;

f) When a party has deserted the spouse for two years or more;

g) In case of a party treating the spouse with cruelty.

Apart from these grounds, the wife can present a petition of divorce on additional grounds. For example, she can file for divorce if her husband has, after marriage, been guilty of rape, bestiality, etc.

Divorce by Mutual Consent : According to Section 10, the grounds we saw above must exist for a party to file for divorce. However, it may so happen that both parties wish to seek divorce mutually. For this purpose, the Parliament amended this Act to insert Section 10A.

According to Section 10A, parties may together mutually file a petition for divorce in the District Court. In order to do this, they must have lived separately for two years and must be unable to live together. In case parties do not withdraw this petition between 6 to 18 months, the court may dissolve their marriage.

Nullity of Marriage : Apart from the dissolution of marriage, the Act also contains provisions for nullity. Either the husband or the wife may file a petition for this before the District Court. There are a few grounds for which a party may file such a petition.

For example, the impotency or lunacy of a party at the time of marriage can be ground. One can also file this petition if the other party was still married to his/her former spouse during the marriage.

Restitution of Conjugal Rights : The Act also contains a provision for restitution of conjugal rights under Section 32. Under this provision, a party may seek restitution if his/her spouse withdraws from their company. Under restitution, the marriage remains but both parties do not possess all marital rights temporarily.

Custody of Children : The Divorce Act contains some provisions governing custody of children in cases of dissolution or nullity of marriage. Section 41 empowers courts to make interim orders with respect to custody. Even after passing a final decree of separation, the court may award custody to any specific party.

Question No. 51

Explain the jurisdiction of the High Courts under the Indian Divorce Act, 1869 ?

Answer :

Matrimonial Jurisdiction of High Courts : Section 4 of the Indian Divorce Act, 1869, the jurisdiction now exercised by the High Courts in respect of divorce a *mensa et toro,* and in all other causes, suits and matters matrimonial, shall be exercised by such courts and by the District Courts subject to the provisions in this Act contained, and not otherwise except so far as relates to the granting of marriage licence which may be granted as if his Act had not been passed.

Enforcement of Decrees or Order made by High Courts : Under Section 5 of the Act, any decree or order of the late Supreme Court of Judicature of Calcutta, Madras or Bombay sitting on the ecclesiastical side, or of any of the said High Courts sitting in the exercise of their matrimonial jurisdiction, respectively, in any cause or matters matrimonial, may be enforced and dealt with by the said High Courts respectively, as hereinafter mentioned, in like manner as if such decree or order has been originally made under this Act by the Court so enforcing or dealing with the same.

Pending Suits : All suits and proceedings in causes and matters matrimonial, which when this Act comes into operation are pending in any High Court, shall be dealt with and decided by such court, so far as may be, as if they had been originally instituted therein under this Act. (Sec. 6).

In Section 7, the Act lays down that courts in all suits and proceedings under the Act shall act and give relief on principles and rules which in the opinion of the court are as nearly as may be conformable to the principles and rules on which the court for divorce and matrimonial causes in England for the time being acts and gives relief. The rule laid down b the House of Lords would provide the principle and rule which Indian courts should apply to cases governed by the Act and standard of proof in divorce cases would therefore be such that if the judge is satisfied beyond reasonable doubt as to the commission of the matrimonial offence he would be satisfied within the meaning of Section 14 of the Act. The two jurisdiction *i.e.;* Matrimonial and criminal are distinct jurisdiction but terms of Section 14 make it clear that when the court is to be satisfied on the evidence in respect of matrimonial offences the guilt must be proved beyond reasonable doubt and it is on that principle that the courts in India would act.

The provision to section 7 of the Indian Divorce Act, 1869 requires that both parties should have professed the Christian religion at the time of the commission of the matrimonial offence. So in a case to which it applies, relief can be had under the Indian Divorce Act in respect of any marriage whether monogamous or not *(Mrs. Premila Khosla vs. Rajnish Kumar Khosla,* AIR 1979 Del. 78 at p. 80).

Extraordinary jurisdiction of High Court : The High Court may, whenever it thinks fit, remove and try and determine as a court of original jurisdiction any suit or proceeding instituted under this Act in the court of any District Judge within the limits of its jurisdiction under this Act. (Section 8).

The Court may, either of its own motion or on the application of any of the parties draw up a statement of the case and refer it, with court's own opinion thereon, to the decision of the Higher Court. (Section 9). If a decree or order has been made, its execution shall be stayed until the receipt of the order of the High Court upon such reference. (Section 9).

Question No. 52

Write a detail note on Nullity of Marriage under the Indian Divorce Act, 1869 ?

Answer :

Nullity of Marriage : Section 18 of the Indian Divorce Act, 1869 deals with petition for decree of nullity. Any husband or wife may present a petition to the District Court or to the High Court, praying that his or her marriage may be declared null and void.

Under Section 10 and 18 of the Act, it is the husband or wife who are alone competent to institute proceedings for divorce and nullity. It therefore appears that a matrimonial status is conferred on them by the mere fact of solemnization of the marriage. The expression 'wife' according to the dictionary means a woman joined in marriage to a man, and according to webster's new International Dictionary, second Edition, defines 'wife' inter alia to mean a woman united to a man in lawful wedlock. Thus, it is clear that the Legislature in its wisdom though fit to give the status of a husband and a wife to such parties postulating by the said term a subsisting marriage. It appears that marriages which may be declared a nullity for contravening the provisions of Section 19 of the Act may be invalid but not necessarily void ab initio. (Mrs. Rose Simpson vs. Binimoy Biswas, AIR 1980 Cal. 214).

Section 19 of the Act deals with the grounds of decree of nullity. A husband or wife can approach the District Court for a declaration on one of the four grounds enumerated in the former part of institution of the suit. The second ground is that the parties are within the prohibited degree of consanguinity or affinity. The third ground is lunacy or idiocy at the time of marriage and the fourth is that one of the spouses should have had an earlier valid marriage which subsists at the time of the impugned marriage. But only the High Court has jurisdiction to declare a marriage null and void on the ground that the consent of the other party was obtained by force or fraud and a decree can be passed only on application by one of the spouses. (*Gabriel Antony vs. Thressya Gracy,* 1988 (1) HLR 263 (Ker.).

Under Section 19 (1) of the Act, a decree for nullity of marriage can e made if it is proved that the respondent was impotent at the time of the marriage and at the time of the presentation of the petition.

Every decree of nullity of marriage made by a District Judge shall be subject to confirmation by the High Court.

Question No. 53

What are the provisions incorporated in the Indian Divorce Act, 1869 relating to Damages and Costs ?

Answer :

Damages and Costs : Any husband may, either in a petition for dissolution of marriage or for judicial separation, or in a petition to the District Court or the High Court limited to such object only, claim damages from any person on the ground of his having committed adultery with the wife of such petitioner.

Such petition shall be served on the alleged adulterer and the wife unless the court dispenses with such service, or directs some other service to be substituted.

The damages to be recovered on any such petition shall be ascertained by the said court, although the respondents or either or them may not appear.

After the decision has been given, the court may direct in what manner such damages shall be paid or applied.

According to Section 34 of the Indian Divorce Act, 1869 compensation is given to the husband for the loss which he has sustained and not punitive damages. In case actual loss or injury suffered by the husband on account of the adultery is not established, the husband is not entitled to damages. in the case of award of damages to the husband from the adulterer, it is necessary to consider the circumstances of the married life of the husband and the wife from the beginning. But in the case of *B.B. Charles vs. Smt. Nora Banjamin,* (AIR 1979 Raj. 156 at p. 161), the husband had made no avertment for claiming damages from the adulterer. Therefore, it was held that the learned District Judge was not justified in directing the adulterer to pay Rs. 1000/- as damages to the husband under Section 34 of the Act.

Section 35 of the Act deals with the power to order adulterer to pay costs. Whenever in any petition presented by a husband, the alleged adulterer has been made a co-respondent and the adultery has been established the court may order the co-respondent to pay the whole or any part of the cost of proceedings :

Provided that the co-respondent shall not be ordered to pay the petitioners costs if the respondent was, at the time of adultery, living apart from her husband and leading the life of a prostitute.

Whenever any application is made under Section 17 of the Act, the court if it thinks that the applicant had no grounds or no sufficient grounds for intervening may order him to pay the whole or any part of the costs occasioned by the application.

Question No. 54

Write about the Christian Marriage Act, 1872 under which how the marriage is solemnized by a Minister of the Church ?

Answer :

Marriage is a universal social institution which controls and regulates the lives of humans. In India, marriage law and procedure varies according to the community to which the couple belongs. The Indian Christian Marriage Act, 1872 (hereinafter referred as the "Act"), which was enacted during the British era, governs the marriage of Indian Christians.

Essentials of valid Marriage

Section 4 of Act specifies that any marriage between Christians, including a marriage where one of the parties is a Christian, must be solemnized according to the provisions of the Act else it shall be considered as void. Thus, a marriage must satisfy the conditions for a valid marriage specified under the Act and must also be solemnized as per the procedure given in the Act.

Section 60 of the Act specifies the following conditions for a valid Christian marriage:

1. The groom must not be below 21 years of age and the bride must not be below 18 years of age;

2. Neither of the parties must have a spouse still living at the time of marriage;

3. The marriage ceremony must take place in presence of the person licensed under section 9 and atleast two credible witnesses.

Persons authorized to solemnize Marriage

Section 5 of the Act provides that a Christian marriage may be solemnized by any of the following persons:

- any person who has received Episcopal ordination in case of which the marriage must be solemnized according to the rules, rites and customs of the church of which he/she is a minister;
- a clergyman of the Church of Scotland in case of which the marriage must be solemnized according to the rules, rites and ceremonies of the Church of Scotland;
- any Minister of Religion licensed under the Act to solemnize marriage;
- by, on in presence of, a Marriage Registrar, appointed under the Act or,
- any person licensed, under section 9 of the Act, to grant certificate of marriages to Christians.

In case where the marriage is being solemnized by a Minister of Religion or a Marriage Registrar, the Act requires certain procedure formalities to be followed such as giving notice of intended marriage and publication of the notice which is followed by declaration by the parties and registration of marriage. However, in case the marriage is being solemnized by a person licensed under section 9 of the Act, the solemnization process is simpler as no procedural formalities are necessary. In such case, the parties are only required to say to each other, in the presence of the licensed person and two credible witnesses, the following or similar words: "*I call upon these persons here present to witness that I,* ***A.B.****, in* *the presence of Almighty God, and in the name of our Lord Jesus Christ, do take thee,* ***C.D.****, to be my lawful wedded wife [or husband]".*

Rules and procedure for solemnization of Marriage : One of the persons intending marriage shall give a notice to the concerned Minister of the church (*i.e.*, churchman) intimating the names of the parties to the marriage and the church or private dwelling where it is to be performed. The notice will be affixed to a conspicuous part of the church by the Minister who officiates in that church. If the marriage is to be performed at a private dwelling, the notice will be affixed in the office of the Marriage Registrar. When one of the persons intending marriage is a minor, the notice must necessarily be affixed in the office of the Marriage Registrar. The father, if he is dead, the guardian, of the person of the minor, and where there is no such guardian, the mother has to give consent to minor's marriage. The Minister of church gives a certificate of Notice received. The marriage should be solemnized within two months thereafter. Otherwise a fresh notice will have to be issued. The marriage when solemnized is registered in the Register of Marriage maintained by the Minister of the Church.

Solemnization of Marriage : Sections 12 to 26 of the Act deal with the process for solemnization of marriage by a Minister of Religion licensed to solemnize marriages under the Act. The process for such solemnization is as follows:

- Notice of marriage – **Section 12** of the Act requires either party to give written notice, in the form contained in First Schedule of the Act, to the concerned Minister by whom the parties want the marriage to be solemnized. The notice must contain name, surname, profession and residence of both parties, time during which concerned party has lived in their dwelling place and the church/ private dwelling where marriage has to be solemnized.

- Publication of notice – In case the parties want their marriage to be solemnized in a church, **Section 13** requires the concerned Minister to get the notice (received under section 12) affixed in some conspicuous part of the concerned church provided that the Minister is entitled to officiate the marriage. In case where the marriage is intended to be solemnized in a private dwelling, **Section 14** requires the Minister to forward the notice to Marriage Registrar of the concerned district for affixation in some conspicuous part of his/her office.

In case where either party to the marriage is a minor, **Section 15** requires the Minister to send a copy of the notice (received under section 12) to the Marriage Registrar or Senior Marriage Registrar of concerned district.

- Procedure of receipt of notice – Upon receipt of any notice under section 14 or 15, **Section 16** of the Act requires the Marriage Registrar to affix the notice in some conspicuous place in his office. On the other hand, the Senior Marriage Registrar is required to forward the notice to each Marriage Registrar in the same district for such affixation.

- Declaration – **Section 18** of the Act requires either party to the marriage to appear personally before the Minister and declare that there is no impediment of kindred or affinity to the marriage and necessary consents, mandated by law, have been obtained in case where either or both parties are minors. **Section 19** requires consent to be taken, for the marriage, from the father and if the father is dead, from the guardian of the minor. If there is no guardian, the minor's mother may give consent to the marriage.

- Issue of certificate – **Section 17** of the Act states that after notice under section 12 has been given to the Minister by either party to the marriage and after either party has made the declaration required under section 18, the Minister shall issue a certificate to the parties indicating the giving of the notice and making of the declaration. The certificate can be issued only after expiry of 4 days from the receipt of notice under section 12 provided that its issue is not forbidden and the parties have proved to the Minister's satisfaction that there is no lawful impediment to issue the certificate. **Section 20** permits all persons, who are authorized to give consent under section 19, to prohibit issue of certificate under sec. 17 by giving written notice to the Minister. **Section 21** states that if a notice has been given under section 20, the Minister cannot issue a certificate unless he/ she is satisfied, upon examination, that the person prohibiting the marriage is not authorized to do so.

- Issue of certificate to Indian Christians – Section 3 of the Act defines Indian Christians to mean Christian descendants of natives of India. **Section 23** of the Act states that when any Indian Christian gives notice to Minister under section 12 or applies for issuing a certificate under section 17, the Minister shall, before issuing the certificate, ascertain whether the concerned Indian Christian is cognizant of the purport and effect of the notice/certificate.

- Form of certificate – **Section 24** of the Act requires the certificate issued under section 17 to be in the form contained in Second Schedule to the Act.

- Solemnization of marriage – **Section 25** of the Act states that after issue of certificate under section 17, the Minister is entitled to solemnize the marriage between the parties, in the presence of two witnesses, according to such form or ceremony as the Minister may see fit to adopt. **Section 26** of the Act states that if the marriage is not solemnized within 2 months from the date of issuance of certificate under section 17, the certificate shall become void and the parties would not be entitled to get the marriage solemnized without getting a fresh certificate issued under section 17.

The Act does not specify any grounds for dissolution of marriage. The dissolution of a Christian marriage is governed by the provisions of Indian Divorce Act, 1869.

Question No. 55

Write the procedure of solemnization of Parsi's Marriage ?

Answer :

The Parsi Marriage is also regarded as a contract through a religious ceremony of *Ashirvad* is necessary for its validity. 'Ashirvad' literally means blessings. A prayer or divine exhortation to the parties to observe their marital obligations with faith.

Procedure of solemnization of Marriage : For a valid marriage a Parsi should have completed 21 years of age. If a party to the marriage is under that age, the consent of the guardian should be obtained. The plaintiff should not be within prohibited relationship specified in the schedule to the Act. The marriage is solemnized according to a ceremony called "Ashirvad" by a priest. The presence of two other witnesses is also necessary. A Parsi marriage is monogamous. The officiating priest certifies the marriage. The certificate is signed by the priest, the parties to the marriage (or guardian) and the witnesses. It is sent by the priest with a prescribed fee paid by the husband to the Registrar of Marriages. The Registrar enters the certificate in a Register kept for the purpose. The register is accepted as proof of the statements made therein. A register of divorces is also kept by the Marriage Registrar. When a court passes a decree for divorce, nullity or dissolution of marriage, a copy of the decree is sent to the Registrar and is entered by him in the Register kept for the purpose.

Question No. 56

State the grounds available to a Parsi wife for securing a divorce decree under the Parsi Family Law?

Answer :

The grounds recognized for securing a divorce decree under the Parsi Family Law as follows :—

(1) Defendant wilfully fails to consummate the marriage within one year.

(2) Unsoundness of mind of defendant at the time of marriage and up to the date of the suit. The plaintiff should have been ignorant of defendant's lunacy at time of marriage.

(3) Defendant at the time of marriage was pregnant by some person other than plaintiff. The plaintiff should be ignorant of the defendant's lunacy at the time of marriage.

(4) Defendant committing since the date of the marriage Adultery, Fornication, Bigamy, rape or immoral offence.

(5) Defendant being sentenced to 7 years imprisonment under Indian Penal Code.

(6) Defendant causing grievous hunt to plaintiff with venereal disease. When the plaintiff is a woman, defendant forcing her to a life of prostitution is also a ground for divorce.

(7) Desertion for 3 years.

(8) Decree for Judicial separation or separate maintenance not followed up by marital inter-course for 3 years or more.

(9) Decree for restitution of conjugal rights not complied with for a year or more.

(10) Defendant ceasing to be a Parsi.

Question No. 57

Write a Short note on Uniform Civil Code.

Answer :

Need of Common Civil Code : The preamble of Indian Constitution declalres thus India is a 'Sovereign Socialist Secular Democratic Republic. Article 44 of the Constitution which deals with Directive Principles of State Policy, States "The State shall endeavour to secure for the citizens a uniform Civil Code throughout the territory of India".

A large number of cases (through public interest litigation) came before the supreme Court pleading of the following :

(i) praying for the introduction of uniform civil code; or

(ii) declaring certain enactments relating to family law as unconstitutional;

(iii) to declare Muslim Personal Law which allows polygamy as void, as offending Articles 14 and 15 of the Constitution.

(iv) to declare Muslim Personal Law which enables a Muslim male to give a unilateral talaq to his wife without her consent and without resort to judicial process of courts, as void, offending Articles 13, 14, and 15 of the constitution.

(v) to declare that the mere fact that a muslim husband takes more than one wife is an act of cruelty within the meaning of sub-section (8) of Section 2 of Dissolution of Muslim Marriages Act, 1939.

(vi) to declare Sections 2(2), 5(1) and (iii), 6 and Explanation to Section 30 of the Hindu Succession Act, 1956, as void, as offending Articles 14 and 15 read with Article 13 of the Constitution of India.

In all the cases, the Supreme Court stated at the very outset that the petitions mentioned above did not deserve disposal on the merits, as the issues involved were matters of policy with which the Supreme Court would not ordinarily have concern.

(vii) to declare Section 2 of the Hindu Marriage Act, 1955 as void, offending Articles 14 and 15 of the Constitution of India.

In all the cases, the Supreme Court stated at the very outset that the petitions mentioned above did not desercve disposal on the merits, as the issues involved were matters of policy with which the Supreme Court would not ordinarily have concern.

In *Punnalal Bansilal Patil vs. State of Andhra Pradesh,* [AIR 1996 SC 1023] it was observed that uniform law for all persons be desirable but, its enactment in one go may be counter-productive to the unity of nation.

The court further observes that in pluralist society like India, in which people have faith intheir respective religious beliefs or tenets propounded by different religions or their offshoots, the founding fathers, while making the constitution, were confronted with problems to unity and integrate people of INdia professing different religious faiths, born in different castes, creeds or sub-sections in the society, speaking different languages and dialects in different regions and provided a secular constitution to integrate all sections of the society as a united Bharat. The directie principles of the constitution themselves visualise diversity and attempt to foster uniformity among people of different faiths. A uniform law, though it is lightly desirable, enactment thereof in one go perhaps may be couner-productive to unity and integrity of the nation. In a democracy governed by the rule of law, gradual progressive change and order should be brought about. Making law or amendment to a law is a slow process and the legislature attempts to remedy where the need is felt most acute. It would, therefore, be inexpedient and incorect to think that all laws have to be made uniformly applicable to all people in one go. The mischief of defect which is most acute can be remedied by process of law at stages.

SOLVED PRACTICAL QUESTIONS PART - C

Question No. 1

A'a Sunni Muslim dies leaving behind his widow, father, two daughters and two sons. Distribute the property.

Answer :

Facts:

A Sunni Muslim male (**A**) dies leaving behind his **widow**, **father**, **two daughters**, and **two sons**. The question is how his property will devolve according to **Sunni Muslim personal law**.

Issue:

How is the estate of a deceased **Sunni Muslim** to be distributed among the **widow, father, daughters, and sons** under **Muslim Law of Inheritance**?

The **law of inheritance** among **Sunni Muslims** is governed by **Islamic personal law**, particularly the **Shariah**, which classifies heirs into:

1. **Qur'anic heirs (Sharers)** – who get fixed shares.
2. **Residuaries (Asabah)** – who inherit the residue.
3. **Distant kindred** – who inherit only if no sharers or residuaries exist.

Under Sunni law:

- **Widow** (with children): gets **1/8th share**.
- **Father** (with children): gets **1/6th share** as a sharer.
- **Two daughters**: jointly entitled to **1/2 share**.
- **Sons and daughters**: act as **residuaries** for the remaining estate (sons get **double the share of daughters**).

Application:

Let the total property of A be **1 (100%)**.

Step 1: Fixed Shares

- **Widow**: 1/8 = **12.5%**

- **Father**: 1/6 = **16.67%**
- **Two daughters (jointly)**: 1/2 = **50%**

Total fixed shares = 12.5% + 16.67% + 50% = **79.17%**

Residue = 100% " 79.17% = **20.83%**

Step 2: Distribution of Residue among Sons and Daughters

- Residuary heirs: **2 sons** and **2 daughters**
- Ratio of distribution: **2 (per son)** : **1 (per daughter)**

Total parts = 2 + 2 + 1 + 1 = **6 parts**

Each **son** gets:

26×20.83%=6.94%62 ×20.83%=6.94%

Each **daughter** gets:
16×20.83%=3.47%61 ×20.83%=3.47%.

Final Shares:

HeirShare

Widow 12.5%

Father 16.67%

Each Daughter 25% + 3.47% = **28.47%**

Each Son 6.94%.

Conclusion:

Under **Sunni Muslim Law**, the estate of A will be distributed as follows:

- **Widow** – 1/8 (12.5%)
- **Father** – 1/6 (16.67%)
- **Two daughters** – jointly 1/2 (50%) + residue = **28.47% each**
- **Two sons** – from residue = **6.94% each**

This distribution follows the principles of **Shariah inheritance** and reflects the **priority of Qur'anic heirs and residuaries**.

Question No. 2

X'a Sunni Muslim married a Y' a Hindu girl after her conversion to Islam. After a period of 5 years of marriage Y wants to get out of the marriage. What is the way out to Y without going to a court of Law?

Answer :

Issue:

Can **Y**, a converted Muslim woman married to **X**, a Sunni Muslim man, **end the marriage** after five years **without approaching a court of law**? What remedies are available under **Muslim personal law**

Rule:

Under **Sunni Muslim Personal Law**, a woman has certain **non-judicial mechanisms** to seek dissolution of marriage. These include:

1. **Khula – Divorce at the instance of the wife:**

- **Khula** is a form of divorce initiated by the **wife**, where she **offers to return the dower (mahr)** or other agreed consideration to the husband in exchange for her release from the marriage.
- It is based on **mutual consent**, but initiated by the **wife**.
- It **does not require court intervention**, unless the husband refuses.

Essentials of Khula:

- The **wife expresses her desire** to end the marriage.
- She agrees to **return the dower or consideration** taken at the time of marriage.
- The **husband accepts** the Khula request.
- Upon acceptance, the marriage **is dissolved**, and the wife must observe an **iddat** period (waiting period).

2. **Talaq-e-Tafweez (Delegated Divorce):**

- If the **husband had delegated the power of divorce** to the wife in the **nikahnama**, she may pronounce **talaq** on herself.

- However, this is rare and only valid if **such a clause exists**.

3. **Faskh (Judicial Divorce) – Not applicable here unless going to court:**

- Under **Dissolution of Muslim Marriages Act, 1939**, a Muslim woman can approach **court** for divorce on specific grounds (*e.g.,* cruelty, desertion, failure to maintain), but this involves **judicial intervention**, which **Y wants to avoid**.

Relevant Case Law:

- **ShamimAra v. State of U.P. (2002) 7 SCC 518**:

The Supreme Court held that **mere pronouncement of talaq is not sufficient**—it must be reasonable and preceded by attempts at reconciliation.

- **Shah Bano Begum v. Mohd. Ahmed Khan (1985 AIR 945)**:

Though not directly about Khula, this case affirmed that even **divorced Muslim women** are entitled to **maintenance**, shaping the rights of Muslim wives post-divorce.

Application:

In Y's case:

- She is a **converted Muslim**, and her marriage was solemnized **as per Muslim customs**.
- If she wishes to avoid court proceedings, her most viable **non-judicial remedy** is **Khula**.
- She can approach **X**, express her desire for Khula, and **offer to return her mahr**.
- If X agrees, the marriage can be **dissolved amicably** without going to court.
- It is recommended that the Khula be **documented in writing**, in the presence of **religious authorities or witnesses**, and that she observe **iddat**.

Conclusion:

Yes, **Y can dissolve the marriage without going to court** through the **process of Khula**, which is permissible under

Sunni Muslim Law.

- This requires:
  - Her **request** for divorce.
  - Her **willingness to return the dower (mahr)**.
  - The **husband's consent**.

It is advisable for Y to approach a **local Qazi, Shariah council, or religious scholar** to facilitate the process formally and ensure that it complies with Islamic principles.

Question No. 3

A, a Christian die leaving behind a widow, two sons and two daughters. Distribute this Property.

Answer :

Facts:

- **A**, a **Christian male**, dies **intestate** (without a will).
- He is survived by:
  - His **widow**
  - **Two sons**
  - **Two daughters**

Issue:

How should A's property be **distributed** among his **widow**, **sons**, and **daughters** under the **Indian Succession Act, 1925**?

Rule:

Applicable Law:

The **Indian Succession Act, 1925**, governs intestate succession for **Christians** in India.

Relevant Provision:

- **Section 33 of the Indian Succession Act, 1925** deals with the rights of the **widow** and **lineal descendants**.

If the intestate (A) leaves a **widow and lineal descendants (children)**, the property shall be distributed as follows:

Ï% The **widow gets one-third (1/3)** of the property.

Ï% The **remaining two-thirds (2/3)** is to be **equally divided among all lineal descendants** (i.e., sons and daughters).

Application:

Let A's **entire property be 1 (100%)**

Ï% **Widow's share** = 1/3 = **33.33%**

Ï% Remaining 2/3 = **66.67%** to be **equally divided among 4 children** (2 sons and 2 daughters)

Ï% Each child's share = 23÷4=212=16=16.67%32 ÷4=122 =61 =16.67%

Conclusion : Under **Section 33 of the Indian Succession Act, 1925**, the property of A will be distributed as follows:

Heir	**Share of Property**
Widow	**1/3** or **33.33%**
Each Son	**1/6** or **16.67%**
Each Daughter	**1/6** or **16.67%**

This distribution ensures **equality among sons and daughters** and is consistent with the principle of **gender-neutral inheritance** under Christian law in India.

Question No. 4

P'a Hindu married 'Q'a Muslim girl in a Marriage function hall as per the Hindu customary ceremonies. After some time, P abandoned Q. Q wants to file a petition for restitution of conjugal rights. Will she be successful?

Answer :

Issue:

Whether **Q**, a **Muslim woman** who married **P**, a **Hindu man**, in a ceremony conducted according to **Hindu customary rites**, can file a **petition for restitution of conjugal rights**, and whether such a petition would be **legally successful**.

Hindu Marriage Act, 1955 (HMA):

- **Section 2** of the Hindu Marriage Act clearly states that it applies only to:
  - Hindus, Buddhists, Jains, and Sikhs.
  - It does **not apply to Muslims**, Christians, Parsis, or Jews unless they convert to Hinduism.
- **Section 9 – Restitution of Conjugal Rights**:
  - A legally married spouse can petition for restitution of conjugal rights **if the other spouse has withdrawn from the society of the petitioner without reasonable cause**.
  - But this section is applicable only **if the marriage is valid under the Hindu Marriage Act**.

Validity of Marriage under Personal Laws:

- A marriage between a **Hindu and a Muslim** solemnized under **Hindu customary ceremonies** is **not valid under either the Hindu Marriage Act or Muslim personal law**.
- Such an interfaith marriage must be solemnized under the **Special Marriage Act, 1954** to be legally valid.
- If not solemnized under the **Special Marriage Act**, the marriage has **no legal recognition**, and therefore, no statutory remedy like **restitution of conjugal rights** can be claimed.

Relevant Case Law :

- **Sarla Mudgal v. Union of India**, AIR 1995 SC 1531:

  The Supreme Court held that interfaith marriages must be conducted under the **Special Marriage Act** to be legally valid. Marriages under personal laws require both parties to be of the same faith.
- **Lily Thomas v. Union of India**, AIR 2000 SC 1650:

  Reaffirmed that a **marriage between persons of different religions** without conversion and without registration under the **Special Marriage Act** is not valid.

- **ShamimAra v. State of U.P.**, AIR 2002 SC 3551:

  Discussed equitable grounds in Muslim divorce but also reiterated the importance of valid marriage before seeking relief under any personal law.

Application:

- **Q is a Muslim**, and **P is a Hindu**.
- They married **according to Hindu rites**, but **Q did not convert**, and the marriage was **not solemnized under the Special Marriage Act**.
- Hence, the marriage is **not valid** under the **Hindu Marriage Act**, nor is it recognized under **Muslim personal law**.
- Since **Section 9 of the Hindu Marriage Act** applies only to **valid Hindu marriages**, **Q is not entitled** to file a petition under this provision.
- Islamic personal law also does **not provide restitution of conjugal rights** as a statutory remedy.

Conclusion:

No, **Q cannot successfully file a petition for restitution of conjugal rights**, because:

- The marriage is **not valid** under either Hindu or Muslim personal laws.
- It was **not registered under the Special Marriage Act**, which is mandatory for interfaith marriages without conversion.
- **Section 9 of the Hindu Marriage Act** does **not apply** to Muslims or to invalid marriages.

  Q may explore other **legal remedies**, such as:

- Filing for **annulment** or **declaration of void marriage**.
- Seeking **maintenance** under **Section 125 CrPC** if she was dependent on P.

Question No. 5

A Sunni died leaving behind leaving behind his wife, father, mother, full brother.

Answer :

Facts: A Sunni Muslim **dies intestate**, leaving behind the following legal heirs:

- **Wife**
- **Father**
- **Mother**
- **Full Brother**

Issue:

How will the estate of a Sunni Muslim deceased be **distributed among his wife, father, mother, and full brother**according to **Sunni Shariah law**?

Rule:

Under **Sunni Muslim personal law of inheritance**, the property of a male deceased is distributed to **Sharers** and **Residuaries**:

Sharers (entitled to fixed shares):

- **Wife** – 1/8 (when the deceased has surviving descendants; here, there are none '! she gets **1/4**)
- **Father** – 1/6 (but also acts as residuary in absence of descendants)
- **Mother** – 1/6
- **Full Brother** – **Excluded** (blocked) when **father is alive**, as the father absorbs all remaining residue.

Application:

Let the total property be **1 (100%)**

Step 1: Distribution of fixed shares:

- **Wife** – 1/4 = **25%**
- **Mother** – 1/6 = **16.67%**

- **Father** – 1/6 = **16.67%**

  Total of fixed shares = 1/4 + 1/6 + 1/6 = 312 + 212 + 212 = 712123 + 122 + 122 = 127 Step 2: Residue = 5/12 (41.67%)

- **Father**, being a residuary in absence of children, takes the **residue**. So, father's total share = 1/6 (as a sharer) + 5/12 (residue) = 212+512=712=58.33122 +125 =127 =58.33

Note:

The **full brother** is **excluded** from inheritance because the **father is alive** and absorbs the residue.

Conclusion:

The property of A (Sunni Muslim) will be distributed as follows:

Heir	**Share**
Wife	1/4 = 25%
Mother	1/6 = 16.67%
Father	7/12 = 58.33%
Full Brother	**Excluded**

Question No. 6

H married W1 in the year 1980 and lived with her for some time. Due to the cruel behavior of H, W1 left him and started living with her parents. He married W2 in the year 1983 and never look back for W1. W1 filed an application for divorce and maintenance on the grounds of cruelty. He filed a counter petition for Restitution of Conjugal rights against W1. Decide.

Answer :

Facts:

- **H** married **W1** in 1980.
- Due to **cruelty** by H, **W1 left** the matrimonial home and began living with her parents.
- In 1983, H **contracted a second marriage** with **W2** and **abandoned W1**.

- **W1** later filed a petition for **divorce and maintenance** on grounds of cruelty.
- **H filed a counter-petition** for **restitution of conjugal rights** against W1.

Issues:

1. Is **W1 entitled to divorce and maintenance** under Muslim personal law?
2. Is **H entitled to restitution of conjugal rights** despite his second marriage and prior cruelty?

Dissolution of Muslim Marriages Act, 1939 – Section 2:

A Muslim woman is entitled to obtain a **decree for divorce** on various grounds, including:

- **Section 2(viii)(a)** – Husband's **cruelty** (habitual assault, ill-treatment, abusive conduct).
- **Section 2(ii)** – Husband has **neglected or failed to provide maintenance** for two years.

Restitution of Conjugal Rights (RCR):

- Recognized under **Muslim personal law** as a remedy for the husband if the wife **withdraws from his society without reasonable cause**.
- However, if the wife has a **reasonable justification** (e.g., cruelty or second marriage without consent), **RCR cannot be granted**.

Section 125, CrPC (Code of Criminal Procedure):

- A wife, even if divorced, is entitled to **maintenance** if she is **unable to maintain herself**, and the husband **neglects or refuses to maintain her**.

Relevant Case Law:

- **ShamimAra v. State of U.P. (2002) 7 SCC 518**:

  Supreme Court held that **divorce must be validly pronounced** and a husband's mere claim of divorce will not absolve him from liability for **maintenance** unless properly executed.

- **Itwari v. Asghari**, AIR 1960 All 684:

  The court held that **second marriage without first wife's consent**, followed by **cruelty or desertion**, justifies **wife's refusal** to return and entitles her to **maintenance**.

- **SairaBanu v. State of U.P.**, AIR 1999 All 1:

  Affirmed that **cruelty is valid ground** for divorce under Section 2 of the **Dissolution of Muslim Marriages Act**.

Application:

- **W1 left due to cruelty**, which is a **valid ground for divorce** under **Section 2(viii)(a)** of the 1939 Act.
- H's **second marriage** in 1983 without any contact with W1 further strengthens W1's **grounds for divorce and refusal to return**.
- Since **W1 has reasonable cause to withdraw**, **H's petition for restitution of conjugal rights will not succeed**.
- W1 is also entitled to **maintenance**, especially since H **abandoned her** and failed to provide for her.

Conclusion:

W1 is **entitled to a decree of divorce** on the grounds of **cruelty** and **abandonment** under **Section 2 of the Dissolution of Muslim Marriages Act, 1939**.

W1 is also entitled to maintenance under **Section 125 CrPC**, as H failed to maintain her.

H's counter-petition for **restitution of conjugal rights** is **not maintainable**, as **W1's withdrawal was justified** by **cruelty** and **his second marriage**.

Question No. 7

A' gifted his house to his son under a registered gift deed which was accepted by the son.Later on, father cancelled the gift deed unilaterally. Discuss the validity of the gift.

Answer :

Facts:

- **A**, a Muslim father, executed a **registered gift deed** transferring ownership of his **house to his son**.
- The **son accepted** the gift.
- Later, **A unilaterally cancelled the gift deed**.

Issue:

Is the **unilateral cancellation of a valid gift** (hiba) by the **donor (A)legally valid** under **Muslim personal law**, once the **gift was accepted and possession delivered**?

Under **Muslim personal law**, a **valid gift (hiba)** requires the fulfillment of **three essential conditions**:

1. **Declaration (Offer)** – A clear and voluntary intention to gift by the donor.
2. **Acceptance** – Acceptance of the gift by the donee during the lifetime of the donor.
3. **Delivery of Possession** – Actual or constructive delivery of possession of the gifted property.

Once these three elements are satisfied, the **gift becomes complete and irrevocable**, except in specific and narrow circumstances.

Key Principle:

> "A valid gift (hiba) once completed, cannot be revoked by the donor unilaterally."

Relevant Case Law:

- **Abdul Aziz v. Masum Ali**, AIR 1919 PC 132:

  The Privy Council held that a **gift under Muslim law becomes complete and irrevocable** upon:

- Offer,
- Acceptance, and
- Delivery of possession.

- **Mussammat Bakar v. Mussammat Bakar**, AIR 1931 All 562:

  Held that **registration is not essential** under Muslim law, but if it is done, it strengthens the claim of gift.

- **Gulam Abbas v. Haji Kayyum Ali**, AIR 1973 All 246:

  Reiterated that once the gift is validly made with delivery of possession, **even the donor cannot revoke it** without the consent of the donee or a judicial order.

Application:

- In the present case:
  - **Declaration** of gift was made by executing a **registered deed**.
  - **Acceptance** by the son was completed.
  - If **delivery of possession** (actual or constructive) was made, then the gift is **legally complete**.
- As per Muslim law, a gift which satisfies these requirements is **irrevocable**.

  Hence, **A cannot cancel the gift deed unilaterally** unless:

- There is **fraud, coercion, mistake**, or
- The donee is **not in possession**, or
- A court sets aside the gift on valid grounds.

Conclusion:

The **unilateral cancellation** of the gift deed by A is **not valid** under **Muslim personal law**.

Once the **gift is validly made, accepted, and possession is delivered**, it becomes **irrevocable**.

Any cancellation must be based on **recognized legal grounds** and typically requires **judicial intervention**.

Question No. 8

A Muslim wife claims dower from her husband when the divorce takes effect, he objects to the payment of full dower on the ground that the marriage is not consummated. Decide.

Answer :

Facts:

- A **Muslim wife** is seeking **payment of full dower (mahr)** upon divorce.
- The **husband objects**, claiming that the **marriage was not consummated**.
- The issue is whether the **wife is entitled to full dower**, or only a part thereof, due to **non-consummation** of the marriage.

Issue:

Can a **Muslim wife claim full dower** after divorce when the marriage has **not been consummated**, and is the husband's **objection valid** under **Muslim personal law**?

Rule:

1. **Concept of Dower (Mahr) in Muslim Law:**

- **Dower (mahr)** is a **mandatory consideration** in every Muslim marriage.
- It may be **prompt** (payable immediately after marriage) or **deferred** (payable upon divorce or death).
- It is a **legal debt** owed by the husband to the wife.

2. **Effect of Non-Consummation:**

- Under **Sunni law**:
  - If the marriage is **dissolved by the husband** (e.g., through talaq) **before consummation**, the wife is **entitled to half the specified dower**.
  - If the dower was **unspecified**, she is entitled to a **reasonable dower** (*mahr-i-misl*), again **halved**.

- Under **Shia law**:
  - Even if the marriage was not consummated, **full dower** is payable upon divorce unless specifically agreed otherwise.

Relevant Provision:

- The **Muslim Personal Law (Shariat) Application Act, 1937** applies.
- According to classical Islamic jurisprudence, if the marriage is **validly dissolved before consummation**, **only half**of the **specified dower** is payable under Sunni law.

Relevant Case Law:

- **ShamimAra v. State of U.P.**, AIR 2002 SC 3551:

  The Supreme Court reiterated that **dower is a legal obligation**, and the wife is **entitled to claim it as a debt**. However, this case mainly dealt with the **nature of talaq**, not the quantum of dower based on consummation.

- **Nasra Begum v. Rizwan Ali**, AIR 1980 All 220:

  The Allahabad High Court held that **only half of the dower** is payable if the marriage is **not consummated** before divorce, under **Sunni law**.

Application:

- If the parties are **Sunni Muslims**, and the marriage was **not consummated**, and divorce has taken place:

  Ë% The wife is entitled to **half the specified dower**.

- If the dower was **unspecified**, she is entitled to **half of a reasonable dower** (*mahr-i-misl*).
- The husband's **objection to paying full dower** due to non-consummation is **partially valid** under Sunni law.

Conclusion:

If the parties are **Sunni Muslims**, and the **marriage was not consummated**, then:

- The wife is entitled to **half** the **specified dower** under **Muslim personal law**.

. The **husband's objection to paying the full dower is valid**, but **only to the extent** that **full dower is not payable unless** consummation occurred.

Question No. 9

A a Muslim husband pronounced talaq thrice to one of his wives B'. Explain the rights of B under the law.

Answer :

Facts:

Ï% A Muslim husband **pronounces triple talaq** (talaq-e-biddat) to his wife **B** in one sitting.

Ï% The issue is whether this constitutes a **valid divorce**, and what **rights B has under the law**.

Issue:

Whether the **pronouncement of triple talaq** (talaq-e-biddat) by the husband results in a **valid divorce**, and what are the **legal rights of B** following such pronouncement.

Rule:

Traditional Muslim Law (Pre-2017):

Ï% **Triple talaq**, or **talaq-e-biddat**, was traditionally recognized under Sunni Muslim law.

Ï% It allowed a husband to irrevocably divorce his wife by pronouncing "talaq" three times in one sitting, **even without cause or reconciliation**.

Ï% Although considered **legally valid**, it was **widely criticized as arbitrary and unjust**.

ShayaraBano v. Union of India (2017) 9 SCC 1 – Landmark Judgment:

Ï% The **Supreme Court declared triple talaq unconstitutional**, arbitrary, and violative of **Article 14 (equality)** and **Article 21 (right to life and dignity)**.

Ï% Held that **triple talaq has no legal effect**, and a divorce cannot be finalized merely by pronouncing "talaq" thrice in one sitting.

The Muslim Women (Protection of Rights on Marriage) Act, 2019:

- Parliament enacted this law in response to the ShayaraBano case.
- Key provisions:
  - **Section 3**: Pronouncement of triple talaq is **void and illegal**.
  - **Section 4**: It is a **criminal offence**, punishable with **up to 3 years imprisonment and fine**.
  - **Section 5 & 6**: The wife is entitled to:
- **Maintenance** for herself and children.
- **Custody of minor children**, if applicable.

Application:

In this case:

- A **pronounced triple talaq** to B in one sitting.
- As per **Shayara Bano (2017)** and **The Muslim Women (Protection of Rights on Marriage) Act, 2019**, the talaq is:
  - **Void** (no legal effect)
  - **Illegal**
  - **Punishable criminally** under Section 4 of the 2019 Act.

Therefore, **B continues to remain legally married** to A.

She is entitled to:

- **Maintenance** under Section 5 of the 2019 Act (and also under **Section 144 CrPC**, if needed).
- **Custody** of children (Section 6).
- She may also initiate **criminal proceedings** against A.

Conclusion:

The **pronouncement of triple talaq** by A is **null, void, and unconstitutional**.

B retains her legal status as wife and is entitled to:

- **Maintenance**
- **Custody of children**
- **Protection under the 2019 Act**

A may be **prosecuted** and punished under the **Muslim Women (Protection of Rights on Marriage) Act, 2019**.

Question No. 10

X a Muslim wife, Sunni by sect. died leaving behind her husband and two sisters. Distribute X's property.

Answer :

Facts:

- **A**, a Hindu man, is **already married** under the **Hindu Marriage Act, 1955**.
- He **converts to Islam** and subsequently **contracts a second marriage** with a Muslim woman.
- The **first marriage is still subsisting** and has **not been dissolved**.

Issue:

Whether A's **second marriage after converting to Islam**, without dissolving his **first Hindu marriage**, is **legally valid under Indian law**?

Hindu Marriage Act, 1955 – Section 5(i) & Section 17:

- A **valid Hindu marriage** is **monogamous**.
- **Section 5(i)**: A Hindu marriage is valid **only if neither party has a living spouse** at the time of marriage.
- **Section 17**: Bigamy is **punishable** under **Section 82 of the Bharatiya Nyaya Sanhita, 2023** if a person marries again during the lifetime of a spouse.

Bharatiya Nyaya Sanhita, 2023 – Section 82:

"Whoever, having a husband or wife living, marries again without legally dissolving the first marriage, shall be punished with imprisonment up to **seven years and fine**."

Muslim Personal Law (Shariat) Application Act, 1937:

- A **Muslim man** may marry up to **four wives** under **Islamic law**, but **only if he is Muslim at the time of marriage**.
- Islamic law does **not validate** a marriage if it was performed in **violation of prior personal law** obligations.

Leading Case Law:

SarlaMudgal v. Union of India (1995) 3 SCC 635:

- The **Supreme Court** held that:
  - A Hindu husband **cannot escape the monogamy requirement** under Hindu law by **converting to Islam**.
  - The **first marriage remains valid**, and the **second marriage is void** under **Section 82 of the BNS**.
  - The conversion is used **fraudulently** to bypass Hindu law and **does not validate** bigamy.

Lily Thomas v. Union of India (2000) 6 SCC 224:

- Reaffirmed that **conversion to Islam does not dissolve a subsisting Hindu marriage**.
- A second marriage under such circumstances is **void**, and the man is **liable for bigamy** under **Section 82 BNS**.

Application:

- A is **bound by the Hindu Marriage Act**, and his **first marriage is valid and subsisting**.
- His **conversion to Islam** does **not automatically dissolve** the first marriage.
- His **second marriage** without a legal divorce is **void under Indian law** and attracts **criminal liability** under **Section 82 of the Bharatiya Nyaya Sanhita, 2023**.

- The **second wife** may not be entitled to **legal matrimonial rights**, and the **first wife can prosecute** A for **bigamy**.

Conclusion:

A's **second marriage is void** under **Hindu and Indian criminal law**.

He is liable to be **prosecuted for bigamy** under **Section 82 of the BNS, 2023**.

His **first marriage remains legally valid**, and the **first wife** retains all rights under the **Hindu Marriage Act, 1955**.

Question No. 12

P'a Muslim married to Ms. K. Aftera period of 6 years he lost his job and became bankrupt. He divorced his wife. K filled a maintenance case against P. Will he be successful

Answer :

Facts:

- **P**, a **Muslim husband**, was married to **Ms. K.**
- After **six years of marriage**, P **lost his job**, became **bankrupt**, and subsequently **divorced** K.
- K has now filed a **maintenance petition** against P.
- The question is whether K is likely to **succeed in her maintenance claim**.

Issue:

Can a **divorced Muslim woman** (Ms. K) **claim maintenance** from her **ex-husband** (P), who is now **financially bankrupt**, under **Muslim personal law** or **general law**?

Rule:

1. **Muslim Personal Law (Shariat) Application Act, 1937:**

- A Muslim wife is entitled to **maintenance (nafqah)**:
  - **During marriage**; and

- For the period of **iddat** (approximately three months) after divorce.

2. **Shah Bano Case – *Mohd. Ahmed Khan v. Shah Bano Begum,* 1985 AIR 945 (SC):**

- The Supreme Court held that:
  - A **divorced Muslim woman** is entitled to **maintenance beyond iddat**, under **Section 144 BNSS, if she is unable to maintain herself**.
  - The obligation is not restricted to the iddat period **if she has no means of livelihood**.

3. **The Muslim Women (Protection of Rights on Divorce) Act, 1986 – Section 3(1):**

- A divorced woman is entitled to:
  - **Fair and reasonable provision and maintenance** to be made **within the iddat period**.
  - This provision includes maintenance **for the future**, not just during iddat.

4. **DanialLatifi v. Union of India (2001) 7 SCC 740:**

- The Supreme Court **harmonized the 1986 Act with the Shah Bano judgment**, holding that:
  - The **maintenance amount fixed within the iddat period must be sufficient for the woman's entire future**.
  - The husband's **liability does not end with iddat**, though **payment must be arranged within that period**.

5. **Section 144 BNSS:**

- A person who **neglects or refuses to maintain** his **divorced wife** who is **unable to maintain herself** can be ordered to pay **monthly maintenance**, irrespective of religion.

Application:

- P **divorced** Ms. K after becoming **financially insolvent**, but:

- **He is still liable** to make **reasonable and fair provision** for K **within the iddat period**, as per the 1986 Act and **DanialLatifi** case.
- K is **entitled to claim maintenance under Section 144 BNSS** , if she is **unable to maintain herself**.
- P's **bankruptcy** does **not absolve him** of his **legal responsibility** unless he can prove **complete inability to earn** or support even basic maintenance.
- The court will assess **his earning potential** and **other assets or means** before deciding the amount.

Conclusion:

Yes, **Ms. K is entitled to maintenance**, and her **petition is likely to succeed**, based on:

- **Section 3 of the Muslim Women (Protection of Rights on Divorce) Act, 1986**
- **Section 144 BNSS** (as upheld in *Shah Bano* and *DanialLatifi*)
- Her **inability to maintain herself**.

P's **loss of job or bankruptcy** does **not automatically exempt him** from liability; the court may **fix a reasonable amount** based on his **earning capacity** and **future potential**.

---

13. AMuslim marriage is contracted without any Dower fixed by the Parties. Will such marriage be valid? Explain.

Facts:

- A**Muslim marriage** is solemnized **without fixing any dower** (mahr) amount at the time of the marriage.
- The issue is whether such a marriage is **valid** in the absence of a specified dower.

Issue:

Is a **Muslim marriage valid** if **no dower is fixed** at the time of marriage? What are the implications for the wife's rights in such cases?

Essentials of a Valid Muslim Marriage (Nikah):

Under **Muslim personal law**, the essential requirements for a valid marriage are:

- **Offer (Ijab)** and **Acceptance (Qubool)** made in the same meeting.
- **Presence of witnesses** (at least two for Sunni marriages).
- Parties must be **competent** (of sound mind and of age).
- **Dower (Mahr)** is **not a condition precedent** to the validity of the marriage.

Thus, **dower is an incident of marriage, not a condition for its validity**.

Types of Dower:

- **Specified (Mahr-e-Musamma)**: Agreed upon at the time of marriage.
- **Unspecified (Mahr-e-Misl)**: Not fixed, but determined later based on wife's social status, husband's means, and prevailing customs.

Legal Position:

- A marriage **without fixing dower** is **valid**.
- The wife is entitled to **reasonable dower (mahr-e-misl)**, especially:
  - Upon **divorce**,
  - Upon **consummation** of marriage,
  - Or on the **death of the husband**.

Case Law:

A. A. Zanane v. S.B. Zanane, AIR 1968 Bom 112:

- The **Bombay High Court** held that:
  - The **absence of a specified dower** does **not render the marriage invalid**.
  - **Dower can be fixed later**, or the court can determine a **reasonable dower (mahr-e-misl)** if needed.

- The **wife retains the right** to claim such dower even if it was not specified initially.

Application:

- In this case, although the **parties did not fix a dower**, the **essential requirements of a valid Muslim marriage**(offer, acceptance, witnesses, and capacity) were fulfilled.
- Therefore, the marriage is **perfectly valid** under Muslim law.
- The wife is legally entitled to **claim a reasonable dower** if a dispute arises, based on her:
  - Age, lineage, education,
  - Social status,
  - Financial status of the husband,
  - Prevailing customs.

Conclusion:

Yes, a **Muslim marriage without fixing dower** is **valid** under **Muslim personal law**.

The **wife is entitled to mahr-e-misl** (reasonable dower) if dower is not specified.

The **court may fix** such dower in case of **dispute** or on **divorce/ death**.

Question No. 14

A Hindu male converts into Islam and contracts a second marriage, without dissolving the first marriage. Explain the validity of the second marriage

Answer :

Facts:

- A Hindu male **converts to Islam**.
- He **contracts a second marriage** under **Muslim personal law**.

- His **first marriage under Hindu law** is **still subsisting and not legally dissolved**.

Issue:

Is the **second marriage** contracted by a **Hindu male after converting to Islam**, without **dissolving his first Hindu marriage**, **legally valid** in India?

Rule:

Hindu Marriage Act, 1955 – Sections 5(i) & 17:

- Section 5(i): A Hindu marriage is valid only if **neither party has a spouse living** at the time.
- Section 17: A second marriage during the lifetime of the first spouse is **void**, and the person is **punishable** under **Section 82 of the Bharatiya Nyaya Sanhita, 2023** (formerly IPC Section 494 – Bigamy).

Muslim Personal Law (Shariat) Application Act, 1937:

- A Muslim man can marry **up to four wives**, provided he treats them **equitably**.
- However, **conversion to Islam** does not automatically **dissolve a Hindu marriage**.

Constitutional Principle:

- **Conversion** cannot be used as a means to **circumvent personal law obligations**.

Landmark Case Law:

SarlaMudgal v. Union of India, AIR 1995 SC 1531:

- The Supreme Court held that:
  - A **Hindu husband cannot contract a second marriage** after conversion to Islam **without dissolving the first marriage**.
  - The **second marriage is void** under Hindu Marriage Act, and the husband is **guilty of bigamy** under **Section 494 IPC** (now **Section 82 BNS**).
  - Conversion with intent to remarry is **fraudulent and unconstitutional**.

Lily Thomas v. Union of India, (2000) 6 SCC 224:

- Reaffirmed that **conversion does not nullify a valid Hindu marriage**.
- Second marriage without divorce is **void and punishable** under criminal law.

Application:

- A's **first marriage** under **Hindu law** is still **legally valid**.
- His **conversion to Islam** does **not dissolve** that marriage.
- Hence, the **second marriage** is **void under Indian law**, even if it is valid under Muslim personal law.
- He is **liable for prosecution** under **Section 82 of the Bharatiya Nyaya Sanhita, 2023** for **bigamy**.

Conclusion:

A's **second marriage is void** under Indian law.

A is **criminally liable** for **bigamy under Section 82 BNS**.

The **first marriage remains valid and subsisting**, and the first wife can initiate **criminal proceedings**.

Question No. 15

M a Muslim female died leaving her two daughters' father, mother and husband. Distribute her property.

Answer :

Issue:

How should the property of a **Sunni Muslim female (M)** be **distributed** upon her death among her **two daughters, father, mother, and husband**, as per **Muslim personal law**?

Rule:

Under Sunni Muslim law (Faraid), legal heirs are categorized into:

- **Sharers**: Heirs with fixed shares.

Ï% **Residuaries (Asabah)**: Inherit whatever remains after sharers take their due.

Ï% **Distant kindred**: Only inherit in absence of sharers/ residuaries.

In this case:

Ï% All heirs are **Sharers**.

Ï% The distribution is as follows:

Heir	Entitlement
Husband	1/4 (since the deceased has children)
Two Daughters	Together 2/3 (fixed share for two or more daughters when no son exists)
Mother	1/6 (since children survive)
Father	Residuary (will receive the remainder, if any, after distribution to sharers)

Step-by-Step Distribution:

Let the **total estate = 1 (100%)**

Fixed shares:

- **Husband**: 1/4 = 3/12
- **Two Daughters**: 2/3 = 8/12
- **Mother**: 1/6 = 2/12

Total = 3/12 + 8/12 + 2/12 = 13/12 '! Exceeds the estate (overlapping of shares).

Correction by the Doctrine of Awl (Increase):

When fixed shares exceed 1, the estate is adjusted proportionally using the **Doctrine of Awl**.

Total of shares = 13 parts '! Each share is divided by 13

Heir	**Share (out of 13)**	**Percentage**
Husband	3/13	H" 23.08%
Two Daughters	8/13 (jointly)	H" 61.54%
Mother	2/13	H" 15.38%

Father Gets nothing as residuary—nothing is left

Conclusion:

The final distribution of M's estate under Sunni Muslim law is:

Heir	**Share**
Husband	3/13 (23.08%)
Each Daughter	4/13 (30.77%)
Mother	2/13 (15.38%)
Father	No share (nothing remains after sharers)

Landmark Cases On Muslim Law

1. *Mohammed Ahmed vs. Shah Bano and another*, 1985 SCR (3) 844.

Facts of the case revolve around the concept of maintenance and dower. After the divorce of the respondent by way of 'triple talaq'. The issue arose when she demanded maintenance from her husband.In Muslim customs, a woman is entitled to Mehr or dower, which is given to the woman as a mark of respect and the purpose is for the woman to utilise it after the marriage or if her husband passes away.

Issue : *Whether the personal laws or the Code of Criminal Procedure shall apply.*

Held : The case was maintainable before the Apex court because the petition was brought under the provision of Criminal procedure and the court held that the Muslim woman shall be entitled to maintenance even after the 'iddat' period. However, this judgment was overturned by the enactment of legislation *The Muslim Women (Protection of Rights on Divorce), 1986,* which re-emphasised that Muslim men shall not be liable to maintain their wives after the iddat period.

2. *ShayaraBano vs. Union of India and others*, 1985 (2) SCC 556

Facts of the case revolve around a resident of Uttarakhand who represented the plight of several Muslim women. She had an ugly marriage and she was divorced by her husband by way of triple talaq (Talaq-ul-biddat).

Issue : *Whether this practice of triple talaq is unconstitutional because it violates Article 14,19,21 of the Constitution.*

Held : The Supreme court decided that this practice is violative of *Article* 14 because it is only the man in the marriage who can practise it and the woman cannot hence the principle of equality is violated. By the virtue of *Article 19* the woman should have the choice whilst divorce. And *Article 21* ensure right to life with personal liberty.

3. *Danial Latifi and another vs. Union of India,* (2001) 7 SCC 740

Facts of this case were aftermath to the Shah Bano case, where the petitioner filed the petition before the court challenging the Act of the parliament. The Act was passed as the aftermath of the Shah Bano judgment. A Muslim woman protection of rights on divorce Act,1986 was passed which envisaged that the husband in the marriage shall be liable to pay the amount of dower and the maintenance on during the period of 'Iddat' as embedded in the Muslim personal laws after which the husband shall not be liable or responsible to maintain his wife under any circumstances unless he would prefer it.

Issue: *The issue brought before the court was to challenge the said provision enacted which was Section 3 of the Act as unconstitutional and violates Section 14 and 21 of the Constitution.*

Held: The court discussed the arguments which the petitioners brought before the court. He argues that there is no reason to deprive a Muslim woman of enjoying the rights provided for her under the Criminal procedure. And that the woman should be entitled to maintenance from her husband. Hence the court decided in his favour and declared the provision unconstitutional.

4. *Shamim Ara vs. State of U.P.,* (MANU/SC/0850/2002)

Facts of this case involve the appellant who filed for maintenance from her husband for herself and two of her four children on grounds that the husband had deserted her and treated her cruelly. The respondent claimed that dower has already been paid and the husband agreed to pay Rs. 150 per month for the maintenance of the minor child. Hence, the application for maintenance was dismissed and an appeal was filed before the Supreme Court. This appeal deals with the concept of maintenance where the wife was divorced by her husband and was also paid the dower.

***Issue** : Whether the court can order the husband to pay maintenance to the wife when the dower has been paid.*

Held : The Apex court stated that the husband shall be liable to pay maintenance for the two sons they have borne from the marriage and therefore ordered the husband to pay maintenance so that the wife who is in custody of the children can maintain her children.

5. *Sarla Mudgal vs. Union of India,* 1995 AIR 1531

Facts : There were two petitions clubbed by the Supreme court. The basic facts in both these petitions were that the husband flees from the first marriage which was solemnised under the Hindu Marriage Act, 1955. Further, the husband fled and converted into Islam only for the purpose of remarrying thereby by-passing Section 494 of Indian Penal Code that prohibits remarriage while the subsistence of one marriage.

***Issues** : There were two issues before the court*

1. *Whether the second marriage after converting from Hindu to Islam shall be valid.*

2. *Whether the man shall be liable by the virtue of Section 494 of the Indian Penal Code.*

Held : The apex court held that the man is trying to invade the first marriage and leave the wife stranded. Thereby, held that since according to the Hindu Marriage Act, 1955, a man under its provisions cannot have two marriages at a time. It was held by the court that the second marriage shall be void in nature since the first marriage is not dissolved and the conversion which has taken place only to commit fraud and to marry two women at the same time shall hold no good. The conversion shall not be affected but the second marriage shall be void.

6. *Chand Patel vs. Bismillah Begum,* (2008) 4 SCC 774

The facts of the case include the petitioner Chand Begum who filed an application for maintenance before the

Magistrate for herself and her minor daughter on the ground that the respondent-husband married her sister and after which she has been neglected and not maintained.

Issues : *The Supreme Court dealt with the questions of:*

- *Whether marriage of a Muslim man to sisters would be a valid marriage, void marriage or a mere irregular marriage and*
- *Whether the husband will be liable to maintain both the sisters.*

Held : The Supreme court held that the marriage of a man with two sisters shall not be void. It stated that this marriage shall merely be irregular in nature. And further discussed that the child of out such marriage shall be entitled to inheritance from his father. It was further discussed that a marriage in which the wife is Hindu and the child borne out of such marriage shall also have the right over the inheritance. It stated that marriages which have taken place without any witnesses or marriage during the 'iddat' period of the former wife only these are circumstances under which the marriage between the parties can be held to be invalid.

7. *Ahmedabad Women Action Group (AWAG) vs. Union of India,* (1997) 3SCC 573

Facts : This case has been filed by a voluntary organization working for women empowerment as a Public Interest Litigation. It shook the entire nation. The petitioners, in this case, challenged several traditional practices under the Muslim personal law as unconstitutional.

First, the practice of polygamy was alleged to be violative of Article 14 and 15. Second, the practice of the system of unilateral talaq by Muslim husbands as violative of Article 14 and 15. Third, to hold that remarriage during the existence of a marriage by a Muslim husband shall amount to cruelty itself. Last, to hold that the Muslim Women (Protection of Rights on Divorce) Act, 1986 is unconstitutional for violation of Article 14 and 15.

Held : The court observed that this practice can only be followed by the Muslim husband in the marriage and not the woman. Hence, it was also stated that this causes agony and can be a form of cruelty upon the wife. The practice of triple talaq which is a mere saying of the word Talaq causing the dissolution of marriage without giving the woman any resort in court or any other place. Leaving her high and dry when the man decides that he does not want the marriage. This tradition also can only be practised by the husband and not by the wife. The laws of inheritance are discriminatory since it does not apply to the females of the family. And she has no right whatsoever upon the property of her own family and hence, violates of Article 14 and 15 of the Constitution.

8. *Imambandi vs. Mutsaddi,* (1918) 20 Bom.L.R 1022.

Facts : In this case, there was a property in dispute before the Bombay High Court which was claimed by three widows of a Muslim man who died intestate. The petitioner claimed that she was the mother of the child and hence, the legal guardian and therefore, was entitled to the share of the property belonging to the child. This case deals with the concept of guardianship and division of property based on guardianship.

Held : It affirms that the man is the ultimate and sole guardian of the child from the marriage this Muslim law further affirms that the on the death or demise of the man or the father of the child, the mother still is not considered the natural guardian of the child. Whereas, the grandfather or man's father holds the position of natural guardian of the child. And after him, the father's brother then becomes the natural guardian in the absence of grandfather.

So, this case further iterated and re-affirmed that the wife cannot hold the place of a natural guardian in case of a legitimate child.

9. *Gohar Begum Nazma Begum,* (1960) 1 SCR 597

The facts of this case deal with the guardianship of the father in case of an illegitimate child. The petitioner is the mother of an illegitimate child who has filed an application under Section 491 of CrPC to transfer the custody of the child from her husband to her. Illegitimacy of a child is a major issue in Mohammedan law and leads to several legal questions as in this case.

Issues : *The issue here which the court dealt with is whether the husband or the father holds the natural guardianship of the minor illegitimate child under the Mohammedan law.*

Held : Here the court affirmed, that the woman or the wife can be a natural guardian only to the illegitimate child. It affirmed that in case of an illegitimate child the circumstances are different from the legitimate child, here even the woman or the wife can be a natural guardian to the illegitimate child and non-transfer of custody of such child will amount certainly amount to illegal detention of the child under Section 491 CrPC.

10. *Noor Sabha Khatoon vs. Md. Quasim,* AIR 1997 SC 3280

Facts : This case specifically deals with the concept of maintenance of the child born out of the marriage after the divorce between the man and the woman. Md. Quasim was married to Noor Saba and had three children from the marriage. The respondent left the appellant with her three children without divorce and remarried to another woman. Later the wife filed an application under Section 125 CrPC for maintenance of herself and her three children which was allowed. The respondent divorced her and approached the High Court claiming that since he has divorced her, the Muslim Women Protection Act, 1986 shall apply according to which he does not need to maintain his wife and children after two years of their birth.

Issue : *Whether the children out the Muslim marriage shall be entitled to maintenance under the CrPC after the divorce of the couple.*

Held : The court held that the child shall be entitled to demand maintenance under 125 of the Code of Criminal procedure and also from the Muslim Woman (Protection of Rights on Divorce) Act. The father shall be liable to pay maintenance to the son until he attains the age of majority and stabilise himself and provide for himself. Further, the father shall be liable to maintain his daughter till the time she is married.

Multiple Choice Questions (MCQs) And Answers On Muslim And Other Personal Laws

1. A marriage of a Muslim male with a Hindu female is:

   A. valid

   B. void

   C. irregular

   D. none of the above

2. Religion of Islam is essentially

   A. polytheistic

   B. monothestic

   C. paganistic

   D. either (b) or (c) and not (a)

3. Islamic law is formally contained in

   A. Hadith

   B. Quran

   C. ljma and qiyas

   D. all the above

4. A marriage prohibited by reason of difference of religion is:

   A. valid

   B. void

   C. irregular

   D. none of the above

5. Shariat Act, 1937 came into operation on

   A. 4th April 1937

Ans. :--1. (C) 2. (B) 3. (D) 4. (C) 5. (D).

B. 7th January, 1937

C. 7th July, 1937

D. 7th October, 1937

6. Muslim law applies to

A. all persons who are Muslims by conversion

B. all persons who are Muslims by birth

C. all persons who are Muslims either by birth or by conversion

D. all persons who are Muslims by birth only and not to Muslims by conversion

7. In India, if one of the parents is a Muslim, the child is to be treated as

A. belonging to the religion of the father

B. belonging to the religion of the mother

C. belonging to the religion mutually agreed upon by the parents

D. a Muslim

8. How many witnesses are necessary for marriage under hanafi school?

A. 1

B. 2

C. 3

D. 4

9. For a valid Muslim marriage

A. offer and acceptance must be at the same place

B. offer and acceptance must be at the same time

C. offer and acceptance must be at the same time and place

Ans. :--6. (C) 7. (D) 8. (B) 9. (C).

D. offer and acceptance may be at different times and at different places

10. What is the age of puberty for a female in Hanafi law:

A. 11

B. 18

C. 15

D. 16

11. Talaq Ahsan can be pronounced only during:

A. Period of menstruation

B. Tuhr

C. In the presence of wife

D. In the presence of witnesses

12. The essentials of a Muslim marriage do no not include:

A. Valid offer and acceptance by the parties to the marriage

B. The parties to the marriage must offer and accept the offer at one and same meeting

C. The presence of at least two Muslim male witnesses (or one male and two female witnesses) of sound mind and of the age of majority

D. The offer and acceptance of marriage must be carried out by the bride and the bridegroom personally

13 What is the share of single daughter when there is no son under Hanafi Law?

A. half

B. one sixth

C. one third

D. one fourth

Ans. :--10. (C) 11. (B) 12. (D) 13. (A).

14. A Muslim girl aged 17 years was given in marriage by her grandfather and her consent was not sought. The marriage is:

    A. Void

    B. Voidable

    C. Valid

    D. Either void or voidable

15. Which law considers Khula as an irrevocable divorce?:

    A. Shia

    B. Hanafi

    C. Maliki

    D. Shafi

16. The process by which the shares are reduced it is called as:

    A. Doctrine of Aul

    B. Doctrine of Radd

    C. Doctrine of Naskh

    D. Doctrine of Representation

17. which of the following marriages is a void marriage

    A. A marriage with wife's sister after divorcing his wife

    B. A Shia male marrying his wife's aunt

    C. Shia male marrying his wife's niece without his wife's permission

    D. A Sunni male marrying a Christian girl

18. An absence of proper witnesses in a Sunni the marriage makes the marriage

    A. fasid (Irregular)

    B. Batil (void)

Ans. :--14. (A) 15. (B) 16. (A) 17. (C) 18. (A).

C. Sahih (valid)

D. Voidable

19. All the irregular marriages are void under:

A. Hanbali

B. Shafi

C. Shia

D. Hanafi

20. The condition of Tuhr is not applicable if:

A. wife and husband are living separate

B. The wife is beyond the period of menstruation

C. both (a) and (b)

D. none of the above

21. A marriage entered into by a girl while she has not attained puberty under Muslim law is a

A. void marriage

B. valid marriage

C. voidable marriage

D. either (a) or (C)

22. There is no right to pre emption in:

A. Bequest

B. Wakf

C. Sadaqa

D. All the above

23. Option of puberty means

A. A Muslim minor girl married during minority by a guardian has no right to repudiate such marriage on attaining puberty

---

Ans. :--19. (C) 20. (C) 21. (C) 22. (D) 23. (B).

B. a Muslim minor girl married during minority by a guardian has a right to repudiate such marriage on attaining puberty

C. a Muslim minor girl married during minority by a guardian has a right to repudiate such marriage on attaining puberty only with the permission of the court

D. a Muslim minor girl married during minority by a guardian can repudiate such marriage with the consent of her husband

24. The option of puberty' can be exercised by the female before attaining the age of

A. 18 years

B. 21 years

C. 15 years

D. either (a) or (b) or (c)

25. Consummation of marriage before the age of puberty

A. deprives the wife of her option of puberty only under certain circumstances

B. deprives the wife of her option of puberty always

C. does not deprive the wife of her option of puberty

D. either (a) or (b)

26. Reciprocal gifts are called:

A. Ewaz

B. Shufa

C. Musha

D. Ariya

27. Husband married during minority loses his right to repudiate the marriage on

A. cohabitation after attaining majority

Ans. :--24. (A) 25. (C) 26. (A) 27. (C).

B. payment of dower

C. either (a) or (b)

D. neither (a) nor (b)

28. Mere exercise of the option to repudiate the marriage

A. does not severe the marital tie

B. severes the marital tie

C. may severe the marital tie if consented to be the other party

D. either (a) or (c)

29. Zina under Muslim law means:

A. sexual intercourse permitted by law

B. sexual intercourse not permitted by law

C. fornication or adultery

D. both (b) and (c)

30. A Muslim can marry any number of wives not exceeding four. If a Muslim marries a fifth wife, such a marriage shall be

A. irregular

B. valid

C. void

D. either A or C

31. Offspring's of a Muslim woman marrying second husband shall be

A. illegitimate but can be legitimised by subsequent acknowledgement

B. legitimate

C. illegitimate and cannot be legitimized by any subsequent acknowledgement

---

Ans. :--28. (A) 29. (D) 30. (A) 31. (C).

D. either (a) or (b)

32. A Muslim man cannot marry

A. a Jew

B. a Muslim woman

C. a Christian

D. an idolaters or a fire-worshipper

33. Marriage of a Muslim woman with a non Muslim shall be

A. valid

B. either (a) or (b)

C. irregular

D. void

34. On the apostasy of one of the parties to the marriage, a Muslim marriage

A. remains valid

B. stands dissolved automatically

C. becomes irregular

D. stands dissolved after the decree of the court

35. In Muslim Law marriage with a woman prohibited by reason of blood relationship

A. irregular and the issue legitimate

B. valid and the issue legitimate

C. void but the issue legitimate

D. void and the issue illegitimate

36. If the husband dies during Iddat in a revocable divorce, is it necessary to observe the Iddat for death?

A. yes

B. no

Ans. :--32. (D) 33. (D) 34. (B) 35. (D) 36. (A).

C. depends

D. none of the above

37. Moonshee Buzul-Ul-Raheem vs. Luteefut-Oon-Nissa (PC), 1861 is a leading case on:

A. Marriage

B. Khula

C. Zina

D. Zihar

38. An irregular marriage

A. creates mutual rights of inheritance between husband and wife, if the marriage is not consummated

B. creates mutual rights of inheritance between husband and wife if the marriage is consummated

C. does not create mutual rights of inheritance between husband and wife irrespective of whether the marriage is consummated or not

D. does not create mutual rights of inheritance between husband and wife if the marriage is not consummated

39. Which of the following is not a legal effect of a valid Muslims marriage

A. status of woman does not change and she is subject to her own premarital school of law

B. status of woman changes and she subjected to the husband school of law

C. neither the husband nor the wife acquires any interest in the property of the other by reason of marriage

D. Mutual rights of inheritance is established

Ans. :--37. (B) 38. (C) 39. (B).

40. The period of "Iddat" in Muslim law is:

A. The period when Muslim women observe fasting after the death of their husbands

B. The period during which the Muslim women are free to leave their husbands and marry another man

C. The period of limitation during which the Muslim women can claim back the dower from their divorced husbands

D. The period of seclusion to be observed by a Muslim woman whose marriage has been dissolved by divorce or death and during which she has to abstain from marrying another husband

41. If a divorced Muslim woman is pregnant, the period of Iddat is:

A. 3 Lunar months

B. 3 months and 10 days or upto delivery, whichever period is longer

C. 4 months and 10 days or upto delivery whichever period is longer

D. 4 months and 10 days or upto deliver whichever period is shorter

42. Muta marriage is recognised as valid form of marriage in:

A. Only Sunni Law

B. Only Shia Law

C. Both Shia and Sunni Law

D. Neither in Shia nor in Sunni Law

43. Quranic heirs are called:

A. Sharers

B. Distant Kindred

Ans. :--40. (D) 41. (C) 42. (B) 43. (A).

C. Residuaries

D. All the above are Quranic heirs

44. Which among the following articles of the Constitution of india validtes the institution of Wakf?

A. Article 28(a)

B. Article 25 (a)

C. Article 26 (c)

D. Article 27 (c)

45. Under Muslim law right to succession is:

A. Primogeniture

B. Spec successionis

C. either a or b

D. none of the above

46. Under Muslim law there is no right by birth. The statement is:

A. False

B. Partly correct

C. True

D. Depends

47. A muta marriage is dissolved

A. by death

B. ipso-facto by the efflux of the period

C. by hiba-e-muddat

D. either (a) or (b) or (c)

48. Can the magistrate issue warrant for the enforcement of an order passed under section 3 of Muslim Women (Protection of Rights on Divorce) Act, 1986:

A. yes

Ans. :--44. (C) 45. (B) 46. (C) 47. (D) 48. (A).

B. no

C. never

D. none of the above

49. In Wakf the ownership of property is transferred to:

A. Mutawalli

B. Almighty God

C. Manager

D. None of the above

50. The grounds for decree for for dissolution of marriage are provided under section......of The Dissolution of Muslim Marriages Act, 1939:

A. 4

B. 2

C. 5

D. 3

Ans. :--49. (B) 50. (B).

MCQ On Special Marriage Act 1954

1. When did The Special Marriage Act 1954, come into force?
   A. 01 January 1954
   B. 01 January 1955
   C. 01 May 1955
   D. 23 April 1954
2. Which section of The Special Marriage Act 1954 deals with the Powers of Marriage Officers in respect of inquiries?
   A. Section 12 of The Special Marriage Act 1954
   B. Section 9 of The Special Marriage Act 1954
   C. Section 14 of The Special Marriage Act 1954
   D. Section 20 of The Special Marriage Act 1954
3. Which section of The Special Marriage Act 1954 deals with the Procedure for registration_?
   A. Section 16 of The Special Marriage Act 1954
   B. Section 14 of The Special Marriage Act 1954
   C. Section 13 of The Special Marriage Act 1954
   D. Section 18 of The Special Marriage Act 1954
4. Section 25 of The Special Marriage Act 1954 deals with_______?
   A. Rights and disabilities not affected by Act
   B. Voidable marriages
   C. Duty of court in passing decrees
   D. Void marriages
5. Succession to property of parties married under Act, is provided in section___ of The Special Marriage Act 1954
   A. Section 24 of The Special Marriage Act 1954
   B. Section 22 of The Special Marriage Act 1954
   C. Section 21 of The Special Marriage Act 1954
   D. Section 23 of The Special Marriage Act 1954

Ans. :--1. (B) 2. (B) 3. (A) 4. (B) 5. (C).

6. Section 18 of The Special Marriage Act 1954 provides_?
   A. Effect of registration of marriage under this Chapter
   B. Legitimacy of children of void and voidable marriages
   C. Relief for respondent in divorce and other proceedings.
   D. Power of H.C. to make rules regulating the procedure
7. Which section of The Special Marriage Act 1954 deals with the Notice of intended marriage?
   A. Section 7 of The Special Marriage Act 1954
   B. Section 4 of The Special Marriage Act 1954
   C. Section 5 of The Special Marriage Act 1954
   D. Section 9 of The Special Marriage Act 1954
8. Section 12 of The Special Marriage Act 1954 deals with________?
   A. Place and form of solemnization
   B. Conditions relating to solemnization of special marriages.
   C. Marriage Officers
   D. Marriage Notice Book and publication
9. Which section of The Special Marriage Act 1954 deals with the Objection to marriage?
   A. Section 7 of The Special Marriage Act 1954
   B. Section 9 of The Special Marriage Act 1954
   C. Section 4 of The Special Marriage Act 1954
   D. Section 5 of The Special Marriage Act 1954
10. Sec. 10 of The Special Marriage Act 1954 deals with____?
   A. Conditions relating to solemnization of special marriages
   B. Marriage Notice Book and publication
   C. Procedure on receipt of objection by Marriage Officer abroad
   D. Place and form of solemnization

Ans. :--6. (A) 7. (C) 8. (A) 9. (A) 10. (C).

QUESTION PAPERS

FACULTY OF LAW

L.L.B. (3 YDC) I-YEAR II-Semester Examination, May/June 2015

Subject : Law

Paper - II

Family Law - II

Time : 3 hours **Max. Marks : 80**

PART - A (5 x 6 = 30 Marks)

Answer any Five of the following

1. Source of Muslim Law
2. Muta Marriage
3. Dower
4. Talaq
5. Domicle
6. Gift formalities
7. Maintenance of Spouses
8. Guardianship

PART - B (2 x 15 = 30 Marks)

Answer any two of the following

9. Discuss the law relating to maintenance of wife and divorced wife under Muslim law.
10. Define Waqf. Explain essentials and kinds of Waqf.
11. Explain the salient features of Special Marriage Act.
12. Illustrate the doctrine of AUC and RADD.

PART - C (2 x 10 = 20 Marks)

Answer any Two of the following.

13. A Muslim husband and wife while enacting in drama, husband pronounced Talaq thrice. But the couple in reality never wanted to get separated. The Muslim religious head insisted that they should take divorce. Decide.
14. Son of F converted himself to Christian religion. Is S entitled to share in his father's property. Is the daughter of S entitled to succeed to S's father property.
15. P died leaving behind her husband, father, mother, daughter and daughter's daughter. Decide the property according to Sunni and Shia Laws.

16. A Muslim women after talaq pronounced by her husband had been given maintenance only during iddat period. She claimed maintenance under Section 125 of Cr.PC. even after iddat period. Can she make such a claim.

FACULTY OF LAW

B.A. L.L.B., (5 YDC) II-Year IV-Semester/B.B.A. L.L.B. (5 YDC) II - Year IV - Semester Examination, May / June 2016

Subject : LAW

Paper : V Family Law - II (Muslim Law and other Personal Laws)

Time : 3 hours **Max. Marks : 80**

PART - A (5 X 6 = 30 Marks)

Answer any Five of the following :

1. Mahr
2. Acknowledgement of Paternity
3. Mutawalli
4. Conversion to Islam and its effect
5. Sub schools of Sunni Law
6. Sources of Muslim law
7. Different between dower and dowry
8. Codicil

PART - B (2 x 15 = 30 Marks)

Answer any Two of the following.

9. What are the conditions of a Valid Muslim Marriage ? Explain the effects of legal marriage.
10. Define 'dower' and explain various kinds of dower.
11. Critically examine the right of maintenance of a Muslim wife on divorce.
12. Examine the legal inconsistencies in the Special Marriage Act, 1954.

PART - C (2 x 10 = 20 Marks)

Answer any Two of the following.

13. 'A' a Muslim girl was given in marriage by her father when she was ten year old. On attaining puberty, she repudiated the marriage. Husband alleges that she can not repudiate the marriage. How would you decide ?

14. 'Abdul' wants to marry 'Mary', a Christian girl. But she refuses to convert to Islam. Is their marriage valid under Muslim Law.
15. Hussain marries Zarina in 2002. In 2012 he marries Fathima. So, Zarina left the house and started staying with her parents and filed a petition for maintenance under sec. 125 Cr.PC. Decide.
16. 'A', a Christian died at the age of 70 years leaving behind his wife, son, daughter and mother. Distribute the property among these four members.

FACULTY OF LAW

B.A. L.L.B. (5 YDC) bba llb (5 YDC)/B.Com. LL.B. (5 YDC) II-Year IV-Semester Examination, May/June 2017

Subject : Law

Paper - V: Family Law - II

Time : 3 hours **Max. Marks : 80**

PART -A (5 x 6 = 30 Marks)

Write short notes on any FIVE of the following :

1. Schools of Muslim Law
2. Muta Marriage
3. Puberty
4. Prompt dower
5. Acknowledgement of Paternity
6. Mutawalli
7. Hiba
8. Codicil

PARTY - B (2 x 15 = 30 Marks)

Answer any TWO of the following questions

9. Explain different sources of Muslim Law
10. Discuss the salient provisions of the Muslim Women (Protection of Rights on Divorce) Act, 1986.
11. Define Will and discuss the essential requisites of a valid Will under Muslim Law.
12. Explain the salient provisions of the Indian Divorce Act, 1896 with its latest amendments.

PART - C (2 x 10 = 30 Marks)

Answer any TWO of the following questions

13. 'A a Mohammedan widow who retained possession of her husband's properties in exercise of her lien for dower dies

leaving B, her father, as her sole legal heir. Can B succeed to her possession of her husband's properties ?

14. 'A' makes a bequest of a house of Y for live and then to A's heirs absolutely. A dies. Then Y Dies. Can A's heirs have any claim to the house ?
15. A Marries B, a woman undergoing 'iddat' at that time. Subsequently A dies. B claims A's property as his wife.
16. A Muslim wife becomes a Christian. The husband files a suit for restitution of conjugal rights. Can she plead her convention as a defence ?

FACULTY OF LAW

B.A. LL.B. (5 YDC) /B.B.A.LL.B. (5 YDC)/B.Com. LL.B.

(5 YDC) II-Year IV-Semester Examination, August/September, 2018

Subject : LAW

Paper - V : Family Law - II

Time : 3 hours **Max. Marks : 80**

PART - A (5 x 6 = 30 Marks)

Answer any FIVE of the following :

1. Legitimacy of children
2. Mutavalli
3. Waqf
4. Doctrine of Aul
5. Option of Puberty
6. Irregular marriage
7. Talaq-e-tafureez
8. Residuaries

PART - B (2 x 15 = 30 Marks)

Answer any TWO of the following questions :

9. Explain the conditions that render a Muslim marriage void and irregular and what are the effects of such marriage.
10. Discuss the law relating to maintenance of a divorced wife with the help of decided cases.
11. Explain the essentials of Waff. How it is created and revoked ?
12. What is Dower (Mahr) ? Explain the objection and classification.

PART - C (2 x 10 = 20 Marks)

Answer any TWO of the following questions :

13. A Muslim wife become a Christian. The husband files a suit for restitution of conjugal rights. Can she plead her conservation as a defence.

14. A Muslim male dies Intestate learning behind their sons and two daughters. Distribute his property as per Sunni law of succession.

15. A owns a house. He makes a gift of it and of the right to use staircase held by him jointly with the owner of the adjoining house. Is the gift valid.

16. A Mohammedan marries a minor girl who has not yet attained puberty. He such to recover custody of the minor for her mother. Decide.

FACULTY OF LAW

LL.B. (3 YDC)/LL.B. (3 YDC)/Honours) I - Year II-Semester Examination, August/September 2018

Subject : LAW

Paper : V Family Law - II

Time : 3 hours **Max. Marks : 80**

PART - A (5 x 6 = 30 Marks)

Write short notes on any FIVE of the following :

1. Schools of Muslim Law
2. Khula
3. Puberty
4. Will
5. Deferred Dower
6. Iddat Period
7. Legitimacy of Children
8. Mutawali

PART - B (2 x 15 = 30 Marks)

Answer any TWO of the following questions

9. Explain various sources of Muslim Law.
10. Discuss the essential requirements of Muslim Marriage. Distinguish between void, irregular and valid marriages.
11. Explain the law relating to maintenance of a Muslim divorced wife.

12. Explain how the property of a Christian male devolves.

PART - C (2 x 10 = 20 Marks)

Answer any TWO of the following questions :

13. A Muslim marriage is contracted without any Dower fixed by the parties. Will such marriage be valid ? Explain.
14. A Hindu male converts into Islam and contracts a second marriage, without dissolving the first marriage. Explain the validity of the second marriage.
15. 'A' a Muslim Pronounced Talaq for 3 times to one of his wives 'B'. Explain the rights of 'B' under Muslim Law.
16. 'M' a Muslim female died leaving her two daughters, father, mother and husband. Distribute her property.

FACULTY OF LAW

LL.B. (3 YDC)/LL.B. (Honours) (3 YDC) I - Year II-Semester Examination, July/August 2019

Subject : LAW

Paper : II Family Law - II

Time : 3 hours **Max. Marks : 80**

PART - A

(5 x 6 = 30 Marks)

Answer any FIVE of the following :

1. Apostasy
2. Dissolution of marriage
3. Valid marriage
4. Requisites of valid will
5. Prompt dower
6. Acknowledgement of Paternity
7. Disqualification of property succession under Muslim law
8. Maintenance under Special Marriage Act

PART - B

(2 x 15 = 30 Marks)

Answer any TWO of the following

9. Classify various principle schools under the Muslim Law
10. Elucidate on concept of Dower.
11. Define Gift and prerequisites of Gift.
12. Salient features of Waqf Act of 1995

PART - C (2 x 10 = 20 Marks)

Answer any TWO of the following

13. A Hanafi Muslim marries for fifth time to fifth wife. Can children of fifth wife are legitimate and can they inherit the properties and enumerate on validity of marriage. Decide.
14. Sultana married Rahim in 1980. She begot him a girl child in 1981. He nglected the child. Wife filed for maintenance of 500/- for her and 300/- for child under section 125 of Cr.PC before judicial magistrate which was dismissed? What remedies does Sultana and the child have ?
15. A and B were married under Special Marriage Act, 1954. Their marriage was dissolved by decree of divorce in 1958. A wife married C. Disputes arose between A and C. A sought for judicial separation from C on ground of cruelty. C contended their marriage was void? Decide the legality.
16. Mohd. Kasim bequeathed all his property to his grandchild and dies leaving his widow and son. Decide on validity of bequest and the remedies for widow and son.

FACULTY OF LAW

B.A.LL.B. (5 YDC)/BBA LL.B. (5 YDC)/B.Com.LLB (5 YDC) II-Year IV - Semester Examination, July / August 2019

Subject : LAW

Paper : V

Family Law - II (Muslim Law and other Personal Laws)

Time : 3 hours **Max. Marks : 80**

PART - A

(5 x 6 = 30 Marks)

Write short notes on any FIVE

1. Quran as a source of law
2. Muta marriages
3. Iddat
4. Talaq by Tafwid
5. Requirement of a valid wakf
6. Revocation of will
7. equity of Redemption
8. Codicil

PART - B (2 x 15 = 30 Marks)

Answer any TWO of the following

9. Define Nikah. What are the legal incidents of valid Mohammedan marriage ?
10. State the provisions of the dissolution of Muslim Marriage Act, 1939.
11. State the provisions of Mohammedan law relating to guardianship in marriage.
12. Discuss the salient features of Indian Divorce Act, 1869.

PART - C (2 x 10 = 20 Marks)

Answer any TWO of the following

13. A marries B, a woman undergoing Iddat at that time. subsequently A dies. B claims A's property as his wife.
14. A bequeathed his property to his grandson B and C. The property was subject to a martgage. After A's death, sold the entire mortgaged property to the mortgage in satisfaction of the debt. C who was then a minor brings a suit to redeem his half share. How would you decide ?
15. A Sunni Mohammedan dies leaving wife, two daughters, father and mother. Divide the estate among them.
16. A Hindu girl aged 22 marries her maternal uncle's son aged 21 under the Special Marriage Act. What is teh effect of the marriage?

FACULTY OF LAW

LL.B. (3 YDC)/LL.B. (Hons.) (3 YDC) I - Year I Semester Examination, August/September 2019

Subject : LAW

Paper : II Family Law - I (Hindu Law)

Time : 3 hours **Max. Marks : 80**

PART - A (5 x 6 = 30 Marks)

(Short Answer Type)

Note: Answer any FIVE of the following :

1. Testamentary Guardian
2. Maintgenance Pendent Lite
3. Notional Partitiuon
4. Class I heirs
5. Custom as a source of Law

6. Karta
7. Doctrine of Relation Back
8. Ceremonies of Hindu Marriage

PART - B (2 x 15 = 30 Marks)

Answer any TWO of the following

9. What are the various source of Hindu Law ?
10. Discuss the rules of succession to the proeprty of a female Hindu dying intestate.
11. What are the requisites of a valid adoption ?
12. What are the grounds of divorce under the Hindu Marriage Act?

PART - C (2 x 10 = 20 Marks)

Answer any TWO of the following

13. A Hindu aged about 65 years died in the year 2009 leaving behind his daughter and two sons. he was cultivating his 4 acres of agricultural land which was ancestral property. After the demise of Mr. A his daughter claimed a share in that ancestral property. Will she succeed?
14. Karta of a joint family sold a part of the joint family property to perform the marriages of daughters of the joint family. A male member of the family questioned the alienation in the court. Will he succeed?
15. A and B a Hindu husband wife mutually agreed to take divorce under Section 13 B of the Hindu Marriage Act within 3 months of from the date of their marriage. Will they be successful in their attempt?
16. A, a male aged about 10 years has been adopted by B and C, a chilless Hindu couple. After a period of 4 years from the date of adoption the couple begat a male child and started the ill treating the adopted child. Because of such ill treatment, the adopted son abandoned the adopted family and joined his natural parents. discuss the right of A in the property of B and C.

FACULTY OF LAW

B.A. LL.B. (5 YDC)/BBA. LL.B. (5 YDC)/B.Com. LL.B. (5 YDC) II-Year IV-Semester Examination, September, 2021

Subject : LAW

Paper : V Family Law - II

Time : 3 hours **Max. Marks : 80**

PART - A (4 x 10 = 40 Marks)

Note : Answer any Four questions.

1. Sources of Muslim Law
2. Conversion to Islam
3. Void Marriage
4. Modes of Talaq
5. Guardianship under Muslim Law
6. Mutawall
7. Grounds of divorce under IUndian Divorce Act, 1869
8. Domicile

PART - B

Note : Answer any one question (1 x 20 = 20 Marks)

9. Explain the different sources of Muslim Law ?
10. Define 'dower' and explain various kinds of dower.
11. Give a critical view on maintenance of divorced Muslim women.
12. Discuss the salient features of the Indian Succession Act, 1925.

PART - C

Note : Answer any one question (1 x 20 = 20 Marks)

13. X, a Muslim has been sentenced to imprisonment for 7 years in a criminal case. On this ground his wife, Shahbana Begum wants to get Divorce. Decide?
14. A Christian dies leaving a widow, two sons and two daughters. Distribute his estate.
15. Abdul wants to marry, a Christian girl. But she refuses to converft to Islam. Is their marriage valid under Muslim Law.
16. X, a Muslim, acknowledges Y as his legitimate son, subsequently X revokes it. is the revocation valid?

FACULTY OF LAW

LL.B. (Hons.) (3 YDC) II-Semester Examination,

August/September, 2024

Subject : LAW

Paper : II Family Law - II

Time : 3 hours **Max. Marks : 80**

PART - A (5 x 6 = 30 Marks)

Answer any Five of the following questions.

1. Hanafi School
2. Mahr
3. Talaq-e-Hasan
4. Guardianship in Marriage (Jabar)
5. Marz-ul-Maut
6. Kinds of Waqf
7. Doctrine of Rad
8. Testamentary succession under Indian Succession Act.

PART - B

(2 x 15 = 300 Marks)

Answer any Two of the following question

9. Discuss in brief the different sources of Mohammedan law.
10. Define Dower. What are the remedies available to a Muslim wife for unpaid Dower?
11. Define Will and what are the requisites of a valid Will under Muslim Law.
12. Discuss various grounds of divorce under Divorce Act, 1869.

PART - C

(2 x 10 = 20 Marks)

Answer any Two of the following question

13. 'A' a Muslim husband phonounced talaq thrice to his wife 'B'. Explain the rights of 'B' under the law.
14. 'X', a Muslim dies leaving behind his mother and a son's daughter. Distribute his property to his heirs.
15. 'a' a Sunni Muslim has two sons 'B' and 'C', B dies in the life time of A, leaving behind son D Soon after the death of his son, A too dies. Distribute the shape among the heirs.
16. Christian dies leaving behind a widow, two sons and two daughters, Distribute his property.

FACULTY OF LAW

B.A. LL.B. (5 YDC)/B.B.A. LL.B (5 YDC)/B.Com, LL.B (5 YDC)

IV Semester Examination, July/August - 2025

Subject : LAW

Paper : V Family Law - II

Time : 3 hours **Max. Marks : 80**

PART - A (5 x 6 = 30 Marks)

Note :Answer any Five of the following questions.

1. Legal consequences of irregular marriage.
2. Hiba and Wasiyat
3. Muta and its comparison with Sahih marriage
4. Dower as a right
5. Shia Law of inheritance
6. Wilayat-e-Ikhtiyar
7. Waqf by user
8. Special Marriage

PART - B

(2 x 15 = 30 Marks)

Note : Answer any Two question from the following

9. Explain the essentials and effects of Dower (Mahr)
10. Discuss the doctrine of acknowledgment of paternity under Muslim law
11. What are the essentials of a valid gift under Muslim law?
12. Discuss intestate succession among Christians under the Indian Succession Act, 1925.

PART - C

(2 x 10 = 20 Marks)

Note : Answer any Two question from the following

13. Iqbal dies leaving his two wives, two sons, and the daughter Distribute his property as per Muslim law.
14. A Muslim woman executes a will in favour of her sister's son. Is it valid?
15. A married Hindu man converts to Islam and subsequently marries a Muslim woman. What is the legality of the marriage with the muslim woman?
16. A Christian woman dies intestate, leaving her father, husband, two daughters and brother. Distribute her property.